PLEASE, LISTEN TO ME!

Your guide to understanding teenagers and suicide

Marion Crook, B.Sc.N.

Self-Counsel Press
(a division of)
International Self-Counsel Press Ltd.
Canada   U.S.A.

Printed in Canada

First edition: December, 1988; Reprinted: July, 1989
Second edition: October, 1992

Canadian Cataloguing in Publication Data

Crook, Marian, 1941-
   Please listen to me!

(Self-counsel psychology series)
First ed. published as: Every parent's guide to understanding teenagers and suicide.
ISBN 0-88908-544-7

   1. Teenagers — Suicidal behavior.   2. Suicides — Prevention.
I. Title.   II. Title: Every parent's guide to understanding teen-
agers and suicide.   III. Series
HV6546.C74 1992   362.2'8'0835   C92-091538-8

Self-Counsel Press
(a division of)
International Self-Counsel Press Ltd.

1481 Charlotte Road   1704 N. State Street
North Vancouver, B.C.   Bellingham, WA
V7J 1H1   98225

CONTENTS

WORKSHEETS

INTRODUCTION

When yet another teenager, a boy I had known and liked, died in suicide in our small town, I finally realized that this fatal escape was a choice that many teenagers were making. I found it almost impossible to think of young, energetic men and women choosing to die. Michael's parents were ordinary, loving, and conscientious. Why would their child commit suicide? Why would he want to leave them? It didn't make any sense to me — socially or psychologically. What was going on in teen culture? Was teen suicide a problem everywhere or just in the northern community where I lived?

I started looking. The newspapers reported suicide pacts among teens, deaths in other cities, other places. I looked up the statistics. The problem was at least as wide as North America. Then the mother of a young woman, Bobbie, came to see me. Bobbie had died in suicide recently as had her older brother. Bobbie's mother brought me journals, poetry, and notes Bobbie had kept for the four years before her death. Bobbie had been loved and wanted. "Do something," her mother said.

I had been a full-time writer for several years, but I did not feel ready to tackle a problem this large and this important. However, one of my publishers was interested in having me write a book for teenagers, and another publisher was interested in a book for parents. They each felt that the number of teenage suicides was horrendous and the need for information severe. Would I please get on with it?

I interviewed 30 teenagers from Vancouver to Halifax who had attempted suicide. The teens told me why they tried it. Some parents of those teens were abusive and sadistic. Some were indifferent. But some were much like my friends — well-intentioned, sometimes ineffective, bumbling perhaps, but caring. Why did some parents seem to be able to prevent suicide and some unable?

I had a degree in nursing and years of experience with school health programs and "problem" children. I had had hundreds of listening sessions with parents in their homes. I had taught parenting classes and worked at the crisis center. I had had four children, now

28, 21, 20, and 14, but I still felt ignorant. I didn't understand this problem.

The 30 teens I talked to told me what life was like from their perspective — why they tried suicide, how they felt, what they needed. From them I went to adolescent psychologists, survivor workers, and psychiatrists as well as many, many books to understand what role parents play in the lives of these teens. I tried to ask questions, read articles, and listen to advice as if I represented all the parents who were going to read this book. What would you want to know? What did teens want from you? How can you help?

Some of what I found was discouraging: there are thousands of teens who are considering suicide. Some of what I found was encouraging: parents can make a difference. It is possible to prevent suicide — not in all situations, at all times, but in most situations, at some time. It is possible for parents to make changes that leave suicide a very unlikely choice for their teens. This book gives you, the parents, explanations, information, and practical advice on how to help your teenager.

1

WHY WORRY ABOUT YOUR TEENAGER?

Teenage suicide is the second leading cause of death among teenagers (aged 15 to 19) in Canada and the United States. We lose more young people to suicide than to any disease.

When many of us were teenagers, the suicide rate for our age group was relatively low (in 1954 less than 3 males and 2 females per 100,000 population). We did not grow up being aware of the suicidal thoughts of our friends. Most of us weren't subject to thoughts of suicide ourselves. We dealt with boyfriends, girlfriends, tobacco, and alcohol. Some dealt with drugs. But most of us didn't even consider suicide as a final escape. We developed no philosophy, defenses, or coping skills to deal with suicide.

Now our children are growing up in a teen culture that considers suicide an escape from stress, a way of dealing with lack of acceptance or lack of ability to cope, and we, their parents, are unprepared. We have a hard time even thinking about it.

It is vitally important to understand that teens are vulnerable to suicide, that suicide is more socially acceptable to teens than it is to parents, and that it is more likely to occur than parents may have previously considered.

The numbers are so disturbing that it is unwise for us as parents to assume that our children are not considering suicide or that they won't consider it at some time in the future. Suicide is a definite threat to the teenage population. Parents need to understand it and to recognize signs and symptoms.

a. THE STATISTICS

Statistics Canada reports that in 1989 death by suicide for young men aged 15 to 19 accounted for 22.7 deaths per 100,000 total population; for young women aged 15 to 19 the rate was 3.2. In the United States, the statistics given are for young men and women together aged 15 to 24; the rate is 13.3 deaths per 100,000.

Male and female suicide rates were similar (and low) in Canada until the 1940s when the rate of male suicides began to climb faster than that of females. From 1960 to 1974, the suicide rates for 15- to 19-year-olds climbed steadily. In 1974 they ceased to climb and have remained relatively constant since.

Many people blame either economic affluence or hardship for our suicide rate increases. But suicide rates don't rise and fall with economic prosperity. They fluctuate no matter what the economy is doing.

The rates show increasing numbers of suicides among young people, but what they do not show is that suicides are probably under-reported. One reason for this is the difficulty coroners have in deciding with certainty that a death was a suicide. In addition, medical personnel, police officers, and coroners are reluctant to add to a family's grief by labeling the death a suicide. It seems kinder to allow the survivors to escape the social stigma attached to suicide by calling the death accidental.

The official suicide rates are evidence of the magnitude of the problem, but they don't give a complete picture. For every teen who is recorded as completing suicide, many more attempt it. While some attempts are reported and statistically compiled, many are not. A guess accepted by many who work in the field of suicide prevention is that there are a hundred suicide attempts for every one completed suicide in the teen population.

If I were quoting statistics on polio, influenza, or any other disease, I would be able to report massive information and public health prevention programs. But suicide is officially ignored in preventive medicine. In the past, we have given little time, money, or effort to suicide prevention programs. This is starting to change — not in the field of health but in the field of education. Schools are beginning to provide prevention programs.

b. ATTITUDES

1. Historical

In years past, society often approved of suicide. The Bishop of Caesarea (A.D. 260-339) advised his Christian followers to embrace suicide as a form of protest against the government of the time. Throughout history, suicide in certain situations was approved by philosophies such as Cynicism, Epicureanism, and Stoicism as well as Christianity.

Suicide was accepted as reasonable by many cultures, particularly when a person chose suicide to —

- save another's life,
- avoid a great evil, such as a terminal illness,
- defend the country, or
- prove devotion (to husband, emperor, church).

2. Society today

North American culture still approves of choosing to die in some situations. It is still considered noble to sacrifice one's life to save another's, and some people consider it noble to die for their country.

Many people today consider suicide a problem of the mentally disturbed. Therefore, they think, if their child is not mentally disturbed, he or she won't try suicide. This myth is prevalent in North America and Britain and is even offered by some advice columnists as fact. It is true that the suicide rate is higher among the schizophrenic population. It is not true that only mentally disturbed people try suicide.

The myth that one must be disturbed to try suicide was given credence by some religious groups who accused a suicide of sin. The person was considered not guilty if he or she were mentally ill. In some religious groups those who committed suicide "while of sound mind" could not be buried in consecrated ground. Such a designation of sin and guilt was an added grief for the survivors. Out of charity, it became kind and socially correct to consider anyone who had tried suicide to be of "unsound mind" and "sin free" and, therefore, blessed in death. The idea that anyone who committed suicide was mentally unstable spread until it was accepted as fact.

Such attitudes make it even more difficult for parents to consider that their teen might be contemplating suicide. If they know that their teen is not schizophrenic, is not depressed, is not "mentally unsound," then they assume that their child will not attempt suicide. "He's not crazy; he won't try it." Such an assumption is comforting, but it is not realistic.

Sometimes parents don't face the possibility of suicide for their teen because they are afraid that if they consider suicide, learn about it, talk about it, they will give their teen encouragement to try it — that their teen will then see suicide as a choice. *This is not true.* But this is the reason teachers give for not discussing suicide in class and friends give for avoiding conversations about suicide.

Parents worry that if they allow their teen to tell them that he is considering suicide, they will have to do something about it. It seems better not to mention it in the hope that teens won't think of it.

Teenagers already see suicide as a choice. The reticence of the past years has not prevented teenagers from thinking about suicide.

3. Teens today

Teenagers told me they have expanded the scope of social acceptance of suicide and now include the individual's need for escape as a good and sufficient reason to die. In one generation we have gone from a society that generally avoided suicide except in rare circumstances to one that accepts it. This attitude of acceptance will probably stay with this generation of teens as it grows older.

c. THIS BOOK

When I first started this research, I was quite sure that my family, friends, and relations were not vulnerable to suicide. "It didn't run in my family." After my research, I am no longer certain that anyone is programmed with special genetic protection against suicide. All our children are vulnerable.

When I started the research for this book, I knew it was important to ask teenagers what happened in their lives, what made suicide attempts seem necessary, what pressures they felt in their families, at school, or with their friends that made suicide look like a way out.

I had worked at the Vancouver Crisis Centre as a volunteer on the crisis lines. I had worked as a community health nurse and seen many family situations and school situations that were stressful. But I still didn't understand why a teen would want to take his or her life. It seemed so wasteful and unnecessary. So I asked teenagers.

I spent one summer traveling from Vancouver to Calgary, Winnipeg, Toronto, and Halifax, and I asked 30 teens why they had attempted suicide. I put an ad in the paper and asked teens to call me and arrange an interview. I tried to get a cross-section of ages from 13 to 19. We met in fast food restaurants, in their homes, and on park benches.

While we were talking, I concentrated on the person and his or her problems. All but two interviews were one-to-one; all were taped on my recorder with the teen's permission, sometimes with the background noises of restaurant dishes and clattering silverware. I found the teens very frank and open. Sometimes the teen had talked the whole problem over with his or her parents and had had psychiatric help and counseling. Most often he or she had not talked about it, had perhaps discussed it with a friend, but often before talking to me had told no one at all.

The teenagers told me what was important to them, how they viewed their future and their parents, what had happened to make life too hard, why they had tried suicide. I spent four months listening, tape-recording answers. I saw no common socio-economic factors among the 30 teens I interviewed. They did not come from just the lower economic class or exclusively from the higher. They came from homes where both parents worked. They came from homes where one parent worked. They came from single parent homes, from families of two children to families of five children.

The number who were sexually abused fell within Canada's unenviable "average." The number who were physically abused was more than I had anticipated — 15 of the 30 had been hit often. This physical abuse was not confined to any social class. Teens who lived with families who were wealthy were hit as regularly as teens who came from poorer families.

d. WHERE PARENTS FIT IN

At the end of the time I spent interviewing these teenagers, I felt badly in need of some reassurance and help myself. What kind of a parent was I? What was I doing that the teens told me was hard for them? From examining how teens felt about their lives, their futures, their problems, I turned to looking at parents. How are we, the parents, supposed to manage in this turbulent world? Parents are not magicians; we are not extraordinarily talented psychologists. We try. We do our best. Obviously our best in many cases is not good enough. We need to have more understanding of the very real threat of death for our children, of their great fear of rejection by us, and of their need for our help.

Surprisingly, teens told me that their parents were the most important people in their lives. In some ways this was gratifying. In other ways it was terrifying. If we are that important to teenagers, how do we imperfect, well-meaning, ordinary people without psychiatric degrees help our children?

With common sense and love? Well, yes, but they need more than that. They need our understanding, and I found that understanding particularly difficult to give. What did I know about suicide, after all? No one in my class at school when I was a teenager even thought about it. Certainly no one completed it. It seemed important to understand the gravity of the situation. What is the problem in our society?

I found I had been doing a great amount of denial in my own life. I had not even thought of suicide as a choice for my children. Considering the statistical evidence that it certainly seems to be an option for teens, why hadn't I looked at it seriously? Why don't other parents give serious thought to this?

Some parents are understandably overwhelmed by the amount of knowledge they need to raise a child. To keep a child safe, a parent has to teach not only about honesty, diligence, responsibility, and caring, but teach the teen about sexual mores and dangers, about the possibility of abuse from friends and relatives, about how to floss their teeth, treat acne, care for contact lenses, ski safely, swim safely, and avoid being mugged in the park and raped at the beach.

The expectation of being "super-mom" and "super-dad" is crushing. It is easier to deny that our children have any risk of suicide than it is to take on another packet of information and another teaching task.

Today, many parents are also struggling to pay for books, clothes, food, education, music lessons, orthodontic work, and school trips. Often, parents use most of their energy working to financially maintain their family, and they truly have little energy left to devote to a full-time education program with their children. The days are gone when parents spent four hours a day working with their teen cleaning the barn, planting the grain, baking the bread. We don't spend working time together where wisdom and advice can be imparted casually, easily. These days we often have to make an appointment with our teen, sometimes weeks in advance, to spend an hour with her. And then, of course, there is the "couple time" that we need without the children to keep our marriages together.

While I understand the pressures on parents — I have them myself — I am also beginning to understand the pressures on teenagers. They are less well equipped to deal with life, and they need their parents. Parents who are aware of the possibility of suicide for their teens, are aware of the signs that indicate suicide is attractive to them, will be better able to help.

Parents need to understand more about their teen, what typical attitudes are, how vulnerable their teen is to thoughts of suicide, how severe the problem is for their teen, how worthwhile some community helpers are, and how parents, the most important people to teens, can help.

Suicide seems to be related to emotional isolation from family and friends, to lack of coping skills, to the teen's vulnerability to emotional pain as well as to unreasonable family and social expectations.

2

WHY CHOOSE SUICIDE?

Why do teens consider suicide an option? Parents usually do not see their children's lives as bad enough that suicide is a good choice. In fact, most parents think their teenager's life is pretty good.

However, teenagers who consider suicide think life is crushing, that dying must be better than living. Sometimes teens consider suicide for months, even years, before attempting it. They weigh their options and still prefer death.

When I first started interviewing teens, I found it difficult to imagine the feelings of hopelessness they experienced. After they told me over and over that they couldn't see any reason for staying alive, that no one would really miss them if they were gone, that they weren't capable of dealing with life, I realized that what I saw as a reasonable, active, satisfying life for a teenager was not necessarily the way that teens saw it. It took much more effort than I had anticipated to wrench my mind and my imagination from my adult point of view and begin to see life from a teen's perspective.

I'm not sure that as parents we will ever truly view life as teens see it. It is not as important that we agree with their point of view as that we accept it.

It is sometimes very difficult for a parent to know the depth of his or her child's despair. Often the child doesn't know.

Helen is a quiet 18-year-old who had attempted suicide several times. She told me about a party at her house. "Everyone left but one friend. He was sleeping on the couch. I was sitting there and I was carving myself up. He woke up and said, 'What are you doing?' I looked at him and said, 'I just want out. I don't want any of this shit any more.' So he took my knife and left. I went to bed and woke up in the morning, and three spots [she showed me her scarred arms] were still bleeding. So I put myself together and went and talked to someone in management at work. It's like a family down there. That guy listened. He asked me, 'Why?' I don't have an answer to why. I just wanted out."

Helen did not understand why she slipped into despair. "The night I did it in October I was drunk. Pretty drunk. And I couldn't feel anything anyway. But the next morning when I woke up I still had that same feeling. And I went into the living room and I sat down with the butcher knife and I sat there and I stared at it for half an hour. And I don't know, you just go blank. And the only thing that's in your mind is suicide. It's just like a big flashing word. I put the knife back that time."

By North American standards, Helen's parents tried. She was fed, clothed, given an education, and as an adult they gave her a home with them and invited her on vacations. But her father told her during most of her growing years she was stupid and good for nothing. Her mother would not, and still does not, talk about problems. They have convinced Helen that she doesn't matter very much in their lives. "I think my parents care, but they really don't say anything. And I really need to hear it."

I asked her, "What about physical affection? Is there any of that?"

"My Dad will give me a hug. My mother never. They don't seem to care. I work, you know, but sometimes I get short of money and I never ask my parents for it. Mom says, 'Why? Why do you feel it's wrong to ask for it?' I don't know why, but I won't ask. Mom said, 'If you need money you ask. I don't want you stealing things.' I've never stolen anything in my life. I don't know where she gets that idea."

When Helen told me about her parents, I wasn't sure that they didn't love her. But it was obvious that Helen thought they didn't. It seems fatally easy to make a teenager feel rejected.

The teens I talked to felt they were unable to cope — with failure, rejection, indifference. They had not been taught how to deal with pain, and they were confused by it. They thought they were "different" from most teens, weaker, less capable, inadequate where everyone else was adequate, incompetent where everyone else was competent, ignorant where everyone else was informed. They thought they were more sensitive to slights, to criticism, to rejection than other teens.

a. SENSITIVITY TO EMOTIONAL PAIN

Many of us know a teenager who has a difficult home life yet who seems to be resilient and personally ambitious. Is there something different about those teens who cannot rise above their troubles?

They often seem more sensitive to emotional pain, but it is possible that low self-esteem made them more ready to accept blame and, therefore, more easily devastated by life experiences.

Some teens seem more attuned to emotions than others; they pick up feelings and intuitively understand them without having to reason. Their sensitivity may also be their strength because they are more understanding of others, more compassionate. But they are also more vulnerable to rejection and criticism.

b. MENTAL DISTURBANCES

Some teens have the added problem of mental disorders. In the group of thirty teens that I interviewed, one was schizophrenic and two suffered from clinical depression, a medical diagnosis of chemical imbalance. Teens are more vulnerable to suicide in these conditions, but teens considering suicide are not necessarily mentally disturbed. In fact, they are rarely mentally disturbed. Teens say that it isn't the state of their mental health that makes suicide more attractive; it is the state of their relationship with their parents.

The word "depression" often appears in articles and books about suicide. To laypeople depression means the state of being unhappy. To professionals depression means a medical disease of biochemical imbalance that leaves the sufferer in a state of despair.

While teenagers can suffer from clinical depression, it is far less common than it is in adults. It would be wrong to assume that your teen has something that a magic pill can cure. It is far more likely that the depression your teen suffers from is a family problem and can be helped by working out the relationships between family members. When I talk about depression in this book, I am talking about being unhappy. That can be a debilitating, draining, over-whelming feeling, but it is not treated with pills.

c. WHY NOT RUN AWAY?

The teens I interviewed also felt they did not have the competence to survive in the world outside the family. I asked them why they didn't run away if the situation was too hard at home. Generally, they felt they were not capable of living on their own.

Robert said, "I thought about running away several times. I could never follow through with that. I thought it'd be easier trying to lose life in a split second than wasting my time running away from it. I

10

had all kinds of plans, pages of lists. I was going to change my name, just get out, live on my own. I had timetables, plane schedules, costs. I didn't have a lot of money. That's one thing that held me back. But I could have got it if I needed it. I guess I didn't want to run away."

Others told me that running away was too hard. They didn't have the energy it took to deal with the problems of running away. And they had no faith in their ability to handle the world outside their families.

Janet tried suicide when she was 12. "I got suspended from school because I stole some money. My grandmother said, 'Don't think about running away because the police will catch you.' I didn't want to go through what I was going to go through with the principal and everything, so I just took some pills. I thought they were strong but nothing happened. I threw up quite a bit, but nothing happened. I don't think anyone knew I'd done it. I told my girlfriend a long time after, but no one knew at the time I tried it. I talked to absolutely no one."

Janet tried suicide again when she was 17, but this time she did it out of a fierce anger at her grandparents. "Like 'I'm going to be dead soon and you're going to regret everything you've said to me. I'll show you.'"

Teresa also tried suicide several times to hurt her parents. These teenagers can't talk to their parents, so they act. Sometimes teens die in this show of bravado. For some teens what starts as a bid for attention becomes a firm choice of suicide.

"When I was 16, I wanted attention, right? So a few times I really didn't have the intention of dying. Like I'd take a razor and draw some lines on my wrist and then I'd plaster bandages over them. Stuff like that. But when I was 17, I was dead serious about dying. I wanted out."

Amy was 19 when I interviewed her. She had survived definite rejection from her parents at 13 when they stopped supporting her financially. With periodic help from her grandmother she survived a life on the streets. I asked her why she tried suicide.

"I didn't think there was anything else to try. I felt lost. I was staying downstairs with my boyfriend's mother. He was a jerk. He didn't talk to me for days and it didn't look like I was going to have a place to stay. My dad just left my mom and neither one of them was going to take me. My dad couldn't and my mom wouldn't. I figured, 'Okay. that's it.' I was 16."

d. IS THERE A PLACE FOR TEENS IN SOCIETY?

The teenagers I talked to felt there was no place for them — no place they were welcome, wanted, or even tolerated, so suicide seemed the only safe place. At the time they tried suicide, they suffered from a grave loss of self-esteem. They felt worthless.

Beth told me, "I never felt good enough. And I was always getting into trouble. Always. There wasn't a day that went by that I wasn't in a fight with my mother. Or I had done something wrong and had to be grounded." It may not have seemed to Beth's parents that she was such a loser, but Beth felt that way. "When you get down, when you start feeling down, everything's a bad dream. You start saying, 'What's there to live for?'"

Suzanne said, "I don't feel important at all. No one really needs me." Yet I found Suzanne's parents thoughtful, respectful of her privacy and, in many ways, trying very hard to help her. But she had been convinced, when she made her suicide attempts, that no one cared about her, no one would miss her.

At about age 13, teens begin to realize that their parents have expectations for them — scholastic, social, and career expectations. If they have been fulfilling those expectations up to this time, the increased expectations of friends and the perhaps different expectations they have of themselves suddenly become overwhelming. Teens realize that they can't possibly fulfill everyone's dreams, and they feel like failures before they even try. Sometimes, they stop trying and seek a path of few challenges until everyone's expectations drop. Sometimes, they choose to leave all the problems — the certain failures — behind in suicide.

Many of the teens I interviewed did not feel necessary in their families and in society. They saw no place for them at home, no job for them in society, no future. They felt no one in their family depended on them or needed them. Many lived separate lives from their parents, perhaps living in the same house but spending most of the time in their room.

After interviewing all 30 teens, I started to see that they shared feelings of inadequacy, feelings of not belonging in their family or society, feelings of hurt and of anger toward parents. As parents we seemed to be judging, critical, uncaring people. We aren't like that — at least not all of us all of the time — but that is how we may appear to our children.

3

ASSESSING YOUR TEENAGER

a. SUICIDE AND ATTEMPTED SUICIDE — WHAT IS SERIOUS?

It is common both in medical journals and in newspaper stories to distinguish between a "serious" attempt at suicide and an attempt motivated "just for attention." It is common to assume that an attempt "just for attention" is less serious than one in which the person definitely wants to die.

Some hospital forms have a checklist that includes "suicide attempt — no real intent to die." How could a doctor possibly check that one? The patient is highly unlikely to tell the doctor in the emergency room what his problems or intentions are.

Teens who take a bottle of cough syrup because they think it is poison are just as serious about dying as those who shoot themselves. It isn't always possible to judge the gravity of the intention by looking at the teen's acts. There may be strong opposing motivations in teens who wish to die and at the same time hope to be saved.

Often those who make non-fatal attempts at suicide do not care if they die in the attempt. They leave living or dying to chance. Dying sometimes seems like a minor side effect in their escape from the present. Their attitude to living is often ambivalent — they want to live at the same time they want to die. And while they may not be committed to dying, they are not 100% committed to living. While there may be some differences in motivation in teens who use suicide as a "cry for help" and those who have decided to die, the results can be fatal in both cases. Any kind of suicide attempt tells you that your teen is willing to risk his or her life. All attempts to die are serious.

b. ASSESSING YOUR TEEN'S INTENTIONS

For the majority of teens, suicide can be prevented. Teens are not put on the road to suicide when they are born. They are not genetically predisposed to suicide. They do not inherit the desire to die. They learn to want death because their experiences in life make death seem better than life. Suicide can be prevented. Parents can prevent it. But it takes more understanding, more time, more skills than most of us thought we would ever need.

One of the skills we as parents need is the ability to assess whether our teen is considering suicide. It is hard to be objective about our own child. It seems much easier to analyze and make recommendations to friends about their children than it is to assess our own.

It is also difficult to assess teenagers since they may have masking behaviors that hide what they are thinking. Depressed teenagers aren't always morose. Sometimes they are bright and talkative. We cannot turn our teen over to the local doctor and say, "Fix the problems." We can't even ask our doctor to tell us if our teen is suicidal, because the medical profession is often less informed than parents. We have to learn to understand our teen, noticing what our teen is doing, listening to what our teen is saying, and paying attention to any changes in his or her life.

As parents, we don't approach our children objectively; we have feelings about them. Over the years, we develop habits that may make listening now difficult. And we have feelings of our own to protect. We are vulnerable to hurt from our children, so we often deny what we don't want to know. We may not want to know that our children feel rejected, abandoned, incompetent.

Parents have to ask themselves: "Is my child happy?" Most of us could answer that question fairly accurately. Then, we have to ask: "If my child is not happy, is he or she considering suicide?"

c. WHAT IS HAPPENING INSIDE?

It is hard to assess teens without understanding why they are behaving as they are. When teens feel ignored and rejected, their anger is directed against those who they feel should love them: their parents (or grandparents or stepparents, whoever stands in the position as parents). This produces guilt and makes teens turn their anger and frustration on themselves.

Many of their actions then come from this self-directed anger. Along with their anger is the conviction that they are worthless, so they are constantly trying to deal with feelings of anger, inadequacy, rejection, failure, and incompetence. All the decisions they make in their lives — from which seat to take in class to whether to smoke pot or steal a car — reinforce their conviction that they are "wrong" and "bad."

It is important for us as parents to understand that this wonderful, talented, attractive son or daughter of ours thinks he or she is worthless, truly worthless. It makes no difference that we find this a ludicrous idea that anyone should think this wonderful child is worthless. It makes no difference that we think his or her worth is self-evident.

Teens feel that everyone else has the same experiences and reactions to emotions, and yet that other teens manage to cope. This assessment on their part contributes to their feelings of inadequacy. Parents who point out that other teens manage to cope make teens feel even *more* incompetent.

Much of teen behavior seem inexplicable to parents. Behavior that looks like deliberate attempts to defy authority, parents, school, and society are a teen's way of coping with pressures. It is very hard for parents to get past those behaviors to the problems beneath. If they deal with only the behavior (work on controlling "bad" language, for instance), their teen will only break out in other maladaptive, disruptive behaviors.

Teens may tell lies repeatedly as a short-term protection from criticism. They feel a great need to be safe — from criticism, from ridicule, from pressure. Their disruptive behaviors, or "acting out," may seem random and unrelated until you understand why teens behave that way.

They are operating from a basic need for security and acceptance. This need must be met before the behaviors cease. The need is not always obvious and most often not articulated. Parents have a puzzling array of clues to work out. It is essential to understand that teens don't act out because they *want* to be isolated, anti-social, aggravating, or selfish. They act out because they need emotional support. It is important for parents to understand that they can deal with the cause of the problems, not with the symptoms.

Teens' concept of death is often not one of finality, but of temporary peace. They sometimes imagine that they will feel the satisfaction of calm, orderly peace. They may see themselves in a state of power over the survivors, hovering over the funeral, watching everyone. Some teens see death as an altered state of being, different from life, but still able to be experienced. And a few think of death as a great nothingness, but one that looks better than the problems of the present.

1. Sensitivity

Many teens feel that they have a unique sensitivity to life, that they are particularly vulnerable to stress and pain. Teens need to know they are not alone in their fine-tuned sensitivity. Such sensitivity is not "bad" in itself. Psychologists, psychiatrists, nurses, social workers, teachers, musicians, actors, and writers have this sensitivity. It is an essential quality of their professions. Such sensitivity is a valid part of personality.

Before they try suicide, teenagers develop feelings of hopelessness, helplessness, and emotional isolation. They try to cope with these feelings. They try to make themselves feel more self-assured, more capable. They do this in some common ways.

2. Teens' coping behavior

If your teen will not tell you what is wrong, you may discern the difficulties from his or her appearance, behavior, and choices. Teens trying to cope with depression and a sense of worthlessness show many of the following signs and symptoms.

(a) School failure

Problems in school are often the first sign parents have that teens are in some kind of trouble. Very often school failures cause frustration and anger in parents; we see school failure as lack of will power or lack of application, and not as a symptom that there may be emotional problems. "If she'd just buckle down and get to work, she wouldn't have any problems." Parents need to recognize school failure as a serious sign that their teen is not coping.

School failure reinforces the teen's poor opinion of herself. She doesn't want to fail; she often doesn't know why she is failing. So school is yet another thing that she can't deal with. When parents concentrate on the failure and not on the underlying problem, they are unlikely to be able to help.

(b) Restless activity

Teens may become more agitated, and anxious, and may have episodes of temper. This can be frightening for a parent. A temper tantrum in a six-foot, two-hundred-pound fifteen-year-old is quite different from a temper tantrum in a tiny two-year-old.

Rages can be a teen's way of trying to combat low self-esteem. Teens may show their anger in reckless behavior and minor accidents. Some teenagers react to anger by becoming more vivacious, louder, teasing and joking more, and being verbally vicious.

(c) Eating problems

Teens may show physical symptoms of depression, such as weight loss or even weight gain. Gaining or losing weight may be methods of making themselves "ugly" so that they have an obvious reason for why no one wants to be with them. Teens may also gorge or starve themselves for reasons that are deeper and more difficult to understand, but are related to their low self-esteem.

(d) Sleeping problems

Often teens who are contemplating suicide do not sleep at night. Or they only manage to fall asleep very late and wake up very early. You may hear them wandering around the house at night, or you may find that they know all the late night programs on radio and television. Many troubled teens will also sleep for long periods during the day.

(e) Looking for acceptance

Because teens who are contemplating suicide feel they don't deserve love, or at least that they don't deserve the love of admirable people, they tend to seek out the company of "losers," those who don't fit into the teen culture well, who consider themselves on the fringe of society, who congregate in gangs in order to feel secure, and who indulge in escapist behaviors such as drinking and taking drugs. Often, emotionally shaky teens will deliberately look for situations that label them as "losers." Nothing is expected of losers, and in this group, at least, they feel accepted.

(f) Romantic relationships

Many teens who feel rejected by their parents find a boyfriend or girlfriend in whom they invest all the responsibility for a loving relationship. The teen's need for affection, acceptance, and understanding is forced onto a friend. When the relationship fails, as it may easily do, he can experience a tremendous sense of loss.

(g) Alcohol and drugs

One in three suicides is related to alcohol in some way. A 15-year-old Calgary girl told me, "Alcohol lets your emotions show more. If you get drunk then you . . . you just don't care. I knew two people who killed themselves when they were drunk. If you've even been thinking of it [trying suicide], it becomes much easier when you're drunk."

Teens who are contemplating suicide often increase their alcohol and drug consumption before a suicide attempt. Teens use mind-altering chemicals for the same reasons adults use them. They find peace and relief from anxieties. An 18-year-old girl in Winnipeg told me, "I was into grass, LSD, any kind of pill, uppers, downers — anything that would take me out of the present and put me somewhere else."

(h) Isolation

Teens who find it harder and harder to cope with stress may give up trying and withdraw from life. They withdraw from conversation, don't answer, or don't offer any opinion. They may withdraw physically to their room or into music or television. They may withdraw from their friends and their former activities, sports, clubs, and gangs.

(i) Inability to accept love

A teen who is convinced that he is worthless is highly suspicious of anyone who offers affection. He believes that no one who is admirable would consider him worthy of being friends. Therefore, if he is offered friendship, the other person must have an ulterior motive such as pity or duty. He feels that the abuse heaped on him by parents or teachers is deserved and only to be expected because he is basically "bad." He feels his condition of worthlessness will last forever — that he will never change.

(j) Earned love

In some families, acceptance and love is earned. If you do well in school, go to church, dress "properly," you will be loved. If you don't, you won't be loved. A teen with low self-esteem doesn't try to "earn" parental love because she is sure that she can't. She is convinced that her parents will not love her no matter what she does.

(k) Sexual orientation

In the past, it was acceptable to be uninvolved with the opposite sex until past age 20. Now, teens have to prove their sexual orientations to their peers early in their lives. Often with inadequate information and little concept of how most people feel, teens attempt to sort out the bewildering world of sexual feelings. This pressure to be knowledgeable and competent sexually, coupled with their low self-esteem,

18

makes them anxious and confused about their sexual identity. They are worried that, if they have no involvement with the opposite sex by age 15 or so, they are gay or lesbian or don't have any feelings at all.

The teens I interviewed told me of several incidences in junior high school where rumor convicted them of homosexuality — and this was definitely not an acceptable image. It was confusing and overwhelming to them and impossible to refute. This is not something they found easy to discuss with parents. In many cases, teens were not surprised by this behavior from their peers since they expected ridicule of some kind. Often they didn't consider fighting back.

(l) Perfectionism

Some teens react to stress by trying to become more perfect — getting straight As, winning more ribbons, earning more badges, in a frantic effort to become good enough for their parents or good enough to satisfy their own high standards. They feel constantly inadequate and, no matter how much they achieve, never good enough.

d. NARROWING OPTIONS

Teens are vulnerable to thoughts of suicide when they are trying to cope with fundamental feelings of inadequacy and worthlessness. If they see their options for coping narrowing, they will consider suicide. When their coping behaviors are cut off or no longer work to keep them feeling whole, they will consider suicide. Teens are most vulnerable to thoughts of suicide when they feel they have no one to talk to.

When teens are convinced they are worthless, unacceptable and unlovable, many actions become reasonable. Why dress well when you know you're a loser? Why study when you are going to fail? Why talk to Dad when he hates you and wishes you weren't living in his house? Why spend time with Mom — she'll only complain about grades, clothes, and a messy room.

Teens' apathy and inability to plan is understandable when you know they think they are worthless. They accept sarcasm, nasty comments, blame, and censure as if they deserved them.

4

PARENTAL ATTITUDES

a. PARENTS' INTENTIONS

Most of us start life with our children with a basic desire to do what's best. We are sure that we will be good parents. During their early years we come to know our children, their strengths, their weaknesses. By the time they are 13, we think we have a fairly good understanding of who they are, and, since we care about them, we have some firm ideas about what directions they should take in life. This seems quite normal.

At about 13 years old, children seem to repudiate parents and indicate that parents are unnecessary and irksome. From being the most important people in their lives, we seem to become redundant, suddenly strangers. This child whom we once understood so well is developing ideas and goals that we didn't expect. It helps to understand that our children are trying to become adults, are trying to separate from us, and that the whole process is healthy. It helps to understand that — but not much. It seems so irrational.

Our teens separate from us in a patchy manner — slipping away clearly and suddenly in some areas and clinging like velcro in others. Your son may drive your car as responsibly as you do, keep the oil up, wash and polish it, pay for gas, and at the same time neglect his homework. Or your daughter may be conscientious about her school assignments but never do a household chore unless reminded eight times.

b. TEENS' NEEDS

It helps to understand that our teens still need our support. The teens I interviewed told me that their parents were the strongest influence in their lives, and these were young men and women 13 to 24. They told me over and over, if their parents supported them they would not have tried suicide. If their parents gave them emotional support and acceptance, they could manage the rest of life.

I find that scary. Most of us have no idea that we are so important for so long. This is pressure to be perfect parents, and we can't be perfect. We will let our teens down, not be there when they need us, not listen to them when it is important to listen. The teens I talked to said that their preoccupation with suicide was directly related to their relationship with their parents. We need help to survive this pressure.

1. Fathers

(a) Disappearing fathers

Most of us probably believe that mothers are the most important influence in their children's lives. This is not what the teenagers told me. Both young men and young women expressed a strong need to be close to their fathers. I asked the question, "How do you rate your relationship with your father if 1 is low and 10 is high." Of the 30 I interviewed, 27 told me they had problems dealing with their father (rated 5 or less on the scale).

Fathers who had been important in their lives when children were young seemed to fade from their lives as they got older. Fathers sometimes withdrew because of divorce or separation or increased work away from home; sometimes they withdrew in emotional indifference. They stopped taking the child to special events, or even for a walk. They stopped listening to the child. Many fathers are unsure of what is best for their teens since loud comments and firm directions no longer bring about action. Some fathers think that without this dictatorial role, they have no role.

There is an insidious, unspoken social theory that fathers are less important to children than mothers — that fathers are less emotional, less interested in their children, and by far less competent than mothers. Perhaps fathers believe this and withdraw from their teenagers' lives because they think that they can no longer offer anything. Or perhaps they find teenagers threatening; they are not sure of themselves and don't want challenge from their children. Or perhaps they don't know how to listen.

(b) Expressing affection

It can be difficult for fathers to show physical affection to sons or daughters since society has narrow limits on what is socially acceptable. In this day of sexual abuse awareness, a father hugging his daughter can be suspected of "perverse" activities, and a father hugging his son can be accused of fostering homosexual tendencies.

21

It is all very inhibiting to a father's natural affection. The safest thing sometimes seems to be withdrawal, avoidance, and indifference. Teens view this lack of physical affection as a reversal of feelings. "Dad doesn't hug me any more" means "Dad doesn't love me any more."

If you find hugging your teen inappropriate now, you need to substitute some other sign of affection: smiling or a pat on the shoulder. Don't abandon expressions of affection altogether or your teen will think you have no feelings of affection.

2. Independence

Some fathers (and some mothers) take the attitude that their sons should be thrown out in the world at 13 and "learn to be a man" as they imperfectly remember happening to them. These same fathers guard their daughters with restrictions and censure as if they were vulnerable plants that would die on exposure to life. Neither attitude builds self-esteem. While teens need to separate from their parents, they need to do it gradually, feeling competent in some areas while they risk tackling others.

Fathers need to give support to their sons and daughters in this exploration of the world. Overprotecting or abandoning a teen who is unready for such a severe separation doesn't teach competence. It's more likely to reinforce the teen's opinion of himself or herself as incompetent and incapable of dealing with life.

c. PATTERNS OF PARENTAL COPING

Many of us parents are unprepared for the changes in our children in spite of the example of our friends' children and the warnings of books and magazines. We can't see why they won't just keep getting better: more interesting, more loving, more admirable. We are prepared for our children to make choices, to change. We have brought them up to be independent and to have good judgment, so we are sure they will make choices that we approve.

The trouble is that they very often make choices that don't meet with our approval. They make mistakes that we can't accept — green hair, unsafe sex. It is often very difficult to maintain some kind of emotional support for our teen in the face of behavior and choices that we can't stand. It is very difficult to separate our love and support from our need to control our teen.

Although parents are unique and separate individuals, they share common aspirations and concerns and often tend to act in similar ways when faced with the stress of teenage children. The following are some of the attitudes that teens reported as hard for them to deal with. Most of us have tried some of these ineffectual coping mechanisms, and some of us have allowed these attitudes to become the habits of family interaction.

1. Withdrawal and avoidance

Withdrawal and avoidance occurs when either or both parents remove themselves from conflict. They may state their opinion and then refuse to discuss it; or they may state their rule with the punishing consequences for disobedience; or look hurt, cry, and refuse to talk about the problem. Parents who use this strategy are inflexible.

Parents are often afraid of their own feelings. They do not want a confrontation that may expose their own anger or fear. They may have unexplored, deep feelings of rejection for this child that are hard for them to face. The child may have been an unplanned and unwanted child from the beginning and only tolerated if he or she fit into a prescribed family plan. Or the child may not be living up to the parents' expectations, for example, in intelligence, talents, athletic ability, or even in looks. Or the parents were accepted by their own parents only when they fulfilled certain expectations, and they feel their child should be controlled in the same way.

This results in rejection of the child. Rejection is not rare. Rejection is all too common, either sporadically or as a habit. Parents say that their teen will not talk to them. The teen knows that the parents will not allow an honest opinion. Parents are quick to blame their teen for the rejection, "He is irresponsible." "She is a loser." "He is a punk." "She won't study." Teens say that they feel worthless when they are not accepted by their parents and so look for acceptance elsewhere while parents feel that the teens reject them first.

2. Criticism

Many parents heap criticism on their children: "You'll never be anybody." "You're lazy." "You're ignorant." They even include: "You're a slut." Some parents concentrate on scholastic problems: "You're not trying." "You aren't good enough." Some focus on social incompetence: "Your friends are stupid." "You never have any friends."

It is a rare parent who can claim to never have criticized his or her child. What teens find difficult to deal with is the constant criticism and belittling that tells them clearly their parents do not trust them, do not admire them, and even do not like them. They believe that they will never be good enough for their parents.

Why do parents criticize? We seem to have the erroneous idea that criticism motivates change: If we tell our teen what's wrong with him, he'll change for the better. Rarely do parents see name calling ("You're lazy") and criticism ("Why don't you change?") as rejection. Almost always, that is how teens understand it. Often we are afraid that our teen is not capable of dealing with life and must have our surveillance and control. We may be afraid that if we withdraw our constant direction, the child will fail.

What happens, of course, is that when we tell our teens what's wrong with them, they defend themselves at first and then reject us. If we tell them often enough, they will believe that they are useless, worthless, whatever we have judged them to be. They will believe that they are destined to be incompetent. If their parents do not have faith in them, they have no faith in themselves. From the acceptance of their own worthlessness, it is only a small step to the conviction that suicide is their destiny.

3. Indifference

Sometimes parents find the problem of living with teenagers so difficult that they choose to ignore them. In effect, parents say to their teen, "You are so much trouble, I wish you weren't here." Parents may not say that directly to the teen or even admit it to themselves, but their actions clearly demonstrate it to their teen.

Such parents may be willing to accept the teen in the home as long as they don't have to be involved emotionally. This attitude is not rare in North America. It is even admired. Parents in this situation are often seen as competent parents who are in charge of their home. Their children may seem quiet and obedient and the parents seem to be in charge. Actually, they are not coping with problems, they are trying to isolate themselves from the problems.

Some parents are angry at their teen and angry at the situation they feel caught in. They may feel incompetent to face the teen's problems, so they deal with those feelings of incompetence by deciding that it is the teen's job to look after himself or herself. The only way such parents can cope with the stress of the teen's problems is to emotionally divorce their child.

While indifference may appear to result in a peaceful home life, the problems of the teen's life do not go away. The worry, fears, and crises come to the teens whether the parents are available for help and support or whether they refuse to be involved.

The teen sees indifference as even greater rejection than criticism or abuse. Indeed, indifference can be carried so far that parents ignore suicidal gestures. One teen told me that she stuffed her mouth full of headache pills in front of her parents and they pretended not to see her do it. Several teens told me that they slashed their arms and came to the dinner table with bandages, and no one ever asked about them. These teens judged their parents as uncaring.

Indifference does not negate problems or solve them. It ignores them. A teen needs help in problem-solving. Refusing to be involved is not effective problem-solving.

4. "Special" treatment for "special" teens

Some parents need their teen to be "special," perhaps "learning disabled" or "gifted" or "artistic." The parent then retains control over this special child because the child cannot be expected to deal with life as other teens do. He or she must have a watchdog, a controller.

When the teen years come, parents feel that this child cannot handle the stresses. They lack faith in their teen. When the teen makes mistakes and fails, the parent sees that as a sign of inability and incompetence instead of a sign of the teen's need to learn. They somehow think that the 13-year-old should suddenly have all the ability needed to deal with the coming years and should be immediately successful. They do not understand the teen years as a process of learning to cope.

Sometimes, parents equate control of their child with being a responsible parent. They want their child to be safe so they try to remain in charge. As the child gets older parents may see their prestigious position of "boss" becoming less important and so manipulate the teen to retain control. By labeling their child "special," they justify their actions to themselves.

Teens in this situation feel incompetent. They are not allowed to deal with life on their own terms. If, over the teen years, they have no practice in recovering from failures, they become afraid of the world. They stay with their parents, but they resent the control parents have over them. They resent having to be constantly grateful and often set up an irritating counterplay to parents' activities, enough to annoy but not enough to precipitate confrontation. Parents avoid confrontation unless it is in the form of a directive. They do not want confrontation that involves listening to the teen and being prepared to compromise. They use confrontation only as a way of forcing the teen to conform to their ideas, rules, and "house" laws.

5. Ridicule and teasing

Of course we tease and joke with our children. They often enjoy it. But teasing can be a form of aggression, a disguised attack on the teen. It is one way an adult can attack without taking responsibility for the aggression. One teen told me that life had been particularly miserable for him from age 13 to 15 because his parents criticized him constantly in a teasing way and then told him he was a poor sport when he objected. Again, the parents avoided confrontation, avoided listening and compromising, by making hit and run comments on his personality, habits, and ideas. They attacked verbally, then retreated behind a laugh.

Many parents feel incompetent to deal with the problems teens present. They see some of their teen's problems and think that ridicule will negate the stress and make the problems seem less important. The result can be a teen who feels ignored and humiliated. Ridicule and teasing effectively prevents teens from bringing up their problems. All of us avoid humiliation. Teens certainly won't seek it. If the parents' method of problem-solving is to tease or ridicule then they won't hear about the problems — until the problems are overwhelming. Teens are often very angry at their parents for teasing. Ridiculing the problems doesn't make them disappear or make them hurt less.

6. Obedience

Parents sometimes believe that if their teen obeyed the rules of the house, the teen would turn into a healthy, happy adult. This is a myth based on past generations' experience. Today, only at home is there an authority figure who wields so much power; authority is much more democratic in the outside world. As teens reach adulthood, they become aware that parents do not have the authority they are assuming. Teens begin to see that it is only at home that blind obedience is expected, and they start to rebel. The teen may never challenge the authority directly, but may begin a low-key resistance: not getting up immediately to obey a command or forgetting" to obey rules.

Teens seek autonomy, but they need help achieving it. They will rebel sporadically and often inappropriately. They need areas of autonomy where they can practice making decisions and living with failures.

Parents who demand absolute obedience have a need to control their environment. They lack trust and faith in their children. This lack of faith is difficult to overcome in teen-parent relationships. The parent's faith in the teen is replaced with negative expectations. The teen knows that the parent expects him to fail and consequently does.

7. Religious observance

Some parents demand scrupulous attention to the laws of a religious organization. Such religious rules can be an extension of parental control. To some parents rigid patterns of religious and family life look like guarantees of safety and happiness. They try to keep themselves, their families, and their world safe and the same as they have always been. When people are unable to deal with change, they often try to control the world around them. This gives them a temporary illusion that everything is staying the same. Eventually they lose control and find the changes have occurred without them.

Often, in the process of becoming independent, the teen sees the need to break away from the parents. If the religion of the family is seen by the teen to belong to the parent and not to an unrelated source, he or she may reject the religion as well as the parent.

A family who operates this way is developmentally delayed. Habits of obedience serve young children and give them a feeling of security, but are not adequate for teens. Teens need to develop good judgment and competence in making decisions. They don't develop this if they are unquestionably obedient.

This attitude doesn't solve family problems, it only avoids conflict and serves a parent's need for an orderly life. It doesn't serve the teen's need to develop problem-solving skills.

8. Special roles

In some families, teens are valued only when they fulfill a particular adult role, such as having a university degree, owning a business, having children, or earning a lot of money. Teens are accepted only as long as they play this role. Most children will fulfill parental ambitions if their acceptance is based on this. But the cost to their feelings of worth is sometimes very great.

Most of us will see bits of ourselves in these family patterns. Sometimes we act in one way, sometimes in another. While these are problem patterns that destroy a teen's self-esteem, many of us fall into the patterns only periodically. Sometimes we adopt those patterns from our families of origin because our parents acted that way. All of us can remember saying something to our children, then immediately thinking, "My mother said that. I swore I'd never say that." We often want to change the habits we brought with us from our original families. When we are emotionally stressed we tend to fall into habits of reacting that are not necessarily helpful, just familiar.

That makes us normal. We make mistakes. We try. We do incorporate some of the characteristics of the generation before us. We do operate out of our family of origin. There are some good qualities that come to us from the generation before.

We also habitually react in some ways that are positive and essential for our teen's self-esteem. Part of the reason for examining the negative habits we have is to separate them from the positive ones. We need to know what we are doing that is helpful and what is not.

d. BEING HAPPY

North American culture demands that children be constantly happy. We don't teach children that sadness is part of life, that boredom, irritation, frustration, and anger are all normal states of being, that they pass with time and they even precipitate good changes. Boredom stimulates creativity. Frustration stimulates new ways of doing things. Anger often stimulates change.

Some children feel that they must present a happy facade for their parents, and they develop facial expressions and habits of denial that mask their true feelings. Parents are often reluctant to allow their child a few days of frustration or sadness. We seem to want to make everything better quickly. Prolonged periods of sadness or anger or frustration can be very hard on teens, but periodic bouts of such feelings are part of life. Teens need to experience a range of emotions and they need to work out their own adaptations to these emotions. They need support in their adaptations, not control or direction. They may work out a better method of dealing with anger, for instance, than you or I ever thought of.

It is discouraging to read the list of family attitudes that contribute to a teen's feeling of rejection and hopelessness. We've all had some of these attitudes. Family life seems to be a roller coaster of crises that we are never prepared for — a crisis in one child's life is resolved while a crisis in another child's life develops. Parents aren't perfect; we try. But the teens I talked to impressed on me how important it was that we *do* try. It is forgivable to have tried ineffective, even detrimental, ways of dealing with problems. It is less forgivable to continue with them until your teenager feels rejected and unacceptable.

5

ASSESSING YOUR SITUATION

It is hard to step back from your family and take a look at the relationships that cause you to act and react the way you do. When you step back, you bring with you the ties that bind you to other family members and you can't be truly separate from them. You can try to get a better understanding of how difficult life is for your teens and try to assess the danger to their lives.

It is often hard to define the problems you are having with your teenager. You may sense that your teen is worried or anxious or angry, but be completely ignorant about why he is like that. It is important to look at what your teenager is doing and to try to assess what that means.

a. HAS YOUR TEEN TRIED SUICIDE?

All attempts are included — even those that were obvious "attention getters" since those attempts are strong cries for help and often come before a fatal attempt.

If your daughter stands in front of you and takes 12 headache pills, she is demonstrating many feelings, including her attraction to suicide. Teens often act out what they can't say. Many who try to commit suicide are trying to communicate as much as, if not more than, they are trying to die.

The anger, frustration, and helplessness that parents feel at such a time makes it hard for them to concentrate on what their teenager needs. It's dangerous to dismiss such an attempt as "only an attention getter," or to justify your lack of action by telling yourself that if she were serious about dying she would have taken more pills. She is serious about dying; she told you that by her actions.

There is a myth that those who try suicide with the obvious intention of being stopped by friends and relatives will never kill themselves. This is not true. Those who have already attempted suicide in any fashion are quite likely to commit the fatal act. A teen who has made a suicide attempt needs immediate family help and support. The whole family needs counseling and professional help.

b. THE TYRANNY OF THREATS

In some cases, teens know that their parents are so upset by their threats of suicide that the parents will do almost anything for them. These are the teens who use threats of suicide to control their parents, "If you don't let me go to the dance, I'll kill myself," "Everyone else has a car. If you don't get me a car, I'll jump off the school roof." It is rarely possible for parents in these situations to extradite themselves and their teen without harm.

In these cases, a parent's concern about suicide contributes to the teen's manipulative ploys. But lack of concern about the teen's threats of suicide is dangerous. Professional help is essential. The family needs diagnostic help and supportive treatment from a psychiatrist, psychologist, or family counselor.

c. DOES YOUR TEEN TRY SELF-INJURY?

Many teens who have low self-esteem and are considering the possibility of suicide seem compelled to injure themselves. Several teens I talked to used a knife to carve slash marks on their arms and their stomachs. In many cases, these scars were ignored by their parents. One girl showed me long scars on the inside of her arms. She has had them for years, and her parents have never asked her about them. It doesn't take a psychology degree to understand that a teen who mutilates herself has such low self-esteem she thinks she deserves to be hurt, but it may take a psychologist to help parents deal with it. Parents may think that if they don't pay any attention to slash scars their daughter will stop attacking herself. That may happen.

Sometimes a teen finds help outside the family. But, sometimes, ignoring such mutilations may prompt teens to repeat or increase their self-destructive behavior. Not talking about it tells the teen that parents don't care, that the clear call for help is being ignored.

d. DOES YOUR TEEN TRY ESCAPE?

1. Alcohol

While many teens use alcohol, as their parents do, only at a weekend party surrounded by friends, some teens use alcohol as an habitual escape. Some use it in most social situations, after school, and on weekends. Others use it as a daily escape.

The difference between their parents' good time activities and the teens' need to escape is only one of degree. Most people manage without alcohol except on certain occasions. Teens escaping into alcohol use it often. They may be able to cope with life only if they are under alcohol's influence. This is not only a drinking problem, it is also a symptom of low self-esteem and of self-destructive ideas.

2. Drugs

For many teens, drugs provide a similar escape. Drugs are usually easy to get, and, more importantly, their use is entirely controlled by the person using them. The teen buys the drugs and decides what, how many, and when to take. Using drugs seems to be a pleasurable escape that is entirely at the will and control of the teen.

3. Television

Television is often used as an escape from reality. Many teens spend hours every day watching a fantasy world. The plots of the stories replace the problems of the teen's world. Reality is moved ahead in time. Teens don't have to even think about their own problems until the television program is over, or until the next program is over, or the next one.

Escape into television occupies the present. This pushes coping with life off into the future. Most adults have some understanding of this since they periodically do the same thing. Teens who are suffering from depression or from an inability to cope with life stretch these escape periods until they watch television most of the day.

4. Music

Loud rhythmic music occupies the mind and temporarily drives out reality. I take my son's Walkman to the dentist, put the headphones on and concentrate on the countermelody in a brass ensemble. This focuses my mind on one thing and successfully blocks out the anxieties I have about dentistry.

Music serves somewhat the same purpose for teens. They can concentrate on the music and block out painful reality. Teen culture pushes music that is not enjoyed by adults or young children; the music is theirs and not understood or tolerated by other age groups.

This keeps teens isolated from adults, including parents, and allows them another escape.

5. Daydreaming

Most of the teens I talked with told me that they spent a lot of time daydreaming in the period just before they tried suicide. Daydreaming is another effort by teens to cope with their problems. They mentally remove themselves, drifting away from the present.

6. Skipping school

One study said that 40% of teens who try suicide are not in school the day before they try it. Certainly, many of the teens I talked to only intermittently attended school. As one girl said, "I didn't feel like going to class. That becomes a habit, too. Like I didn't do the homework I was supposed to from the class I missed last week, so I'd better not go to class this week either." The problems that are raised by missing classes are added to the problems the teen already has dealing with life, and school becomes just one more source of tension. When looking for a way to escape tension, skipping school seems a reasonable option.

e. HOW STRONG IS THE INFLUENCE OF FAMILY AND FRIENDS?

It may seem to some parents that teens are not influenced by family at all. Many teens seem uninterested in or reluctant to join family outings. Yet the 30 teens I talked to told me that their families matter — that their relationship with their parents was more important than any other relationship. They were reaching out by developing ties with girlfriends and boyfriends, but these new friends did not make their need for a strong relationship with their parents any less important.

Teens need to hear, repeatedly, that they are valued, accepted, and appreciated by their parents. They do not assume they are loved. They very often assume they are not loved.

Often what teens hear are criticisms and directions that tell them they are not good enough. This is hard for teens to deal with. Parents often show little faith in a teen's abilities to cope, which reinforces the teen's fear that he cannot cope. The parents' motivation is to help their teen by showing him the "right" way. But the teen interprets direction and criticism as lack of faith and lack of trust. "You tell me what to do all the time. You don't think I can think anything out for myself."

1. The extended family

It is sometimes difficult for teens to receive support from relatives because often they are geographically far away. Sometimes families can substitute good friends for relatives. Teens may grow up with their parents' friends close by and can go to these friends for consultation and support when they can't talk to their parents.

Friends, relatives, and neighbors are often uncritical and supportive. They may also have spent years getting to know the teen during outings, vacations, social occasions. Time spent with someone who knows you and admires you promotes confidence and self-esteem.

My husband's mother lived a thousand miles away from our children when they were growing up, but she visited as often as she could and sent birthday and Christmas presents and took care to keep in touch with the children as they grew older. She made each of her grandchildren feel as if they were perfect and exactly the grandchild she always wanted. She never criticized them to anyone and she let them know that she had great faith in them. Her faith was incorporated into their lives as part of their belief in themselves. The more people who convey that attitude to your child, the more likely the child will be to believe in himself or herself.

If you move many times while the children are growing, it's hard to be sure that your children have longstanding relationships with friends or relatives. If there comes a time in your child's life when he or she cannot talk to you, then it is important that there is a group of adult confidants who care. It could make a great deal of difference. Over and over teens told me they needed someone to listen to them. If they are in the habit of talking to friends or relatives, they will have someone who will listen. Think about your family circle, your social circle, and your teen's social circle. Is there anyone he or she feels is a friend? Does your teen spend much time with this friend?

2. Separating from the family

We often complain that we cannot reach our teens, that they are emotionally distant from us because that's the way the kids want it. We may have indicated to the teen that we don't want her in the family any longer, that it is time she left.

34

In anticipation of teens leaving home, parents may force separation on them before they are ready. We may send our son out to get a job before he is capable; send our daughter off to find an apartment before she can cope; make them responsible for all their decisions before they feel they can manage.

Sometimes parents force rules on the teen — you will not yell at your sister; you will be in by ten o'clock; you will clean the basement every week — that are the criteria for remaining in the family. When we do that we force the teen to choose dependence (you will do as you are told) or isolation (you will leave home).

Outside influences are strong influences and are usually not controlled by parents. Some parents have been so involved in their child's life throughout elementary school that they cannot accept the fact that they are no longer the organizers and directors of their teen's life. They try to continue the patterns that served them in those earlier years.

This inability on the part of parents to give their teens room to grow and experience disappointment and failure often results in directives that are ultimatums: "Either you obey our rules or you leave home." The choice for the teen is often no choice at all. Either he is dependent and accepted, or defiant and isolated.

Sometimes parents do not make the choice obvious but withdraw emotionally from their teen until the choice becomes isolation without emotional support at home (unless he is obedient) or isolation without emotional support away from home. This tactic of control by the parents only makes the relationship worse.

The task of the teen is to separate from the family while still feeling emotionally supported. By demanding compliance, insisting that teens do as they are told, parents can force isolation on them. Certainly, teens are unlikely to confide in their parents under these conditions. They can't afford to be honest and straightforward with parents who want to control them.

The task of the teen separating from the family is also the reciprocal task of parents separating from the teen. We may have as much trouble letting go as the teen has in going. It is hard to give up control of your children's lives, especially if they are making what parents see as bad choices.

It is tempting to lean even harder on a teen who is failing in school or who is in other ways making poor choices. Failure is part of the process of learning and teens need to experience it. When teens make mistakes, parents tend to want to take control of their lives again.

Parents find it hard to allow teens to experience failure and to allow them to deal with it on their own terms.

f. HOW STRONG ARE OUTSIDE INFLUENCES?

Parents often assess a teen's friends by their activities; for example, a basketball group is a good influence and a partying group is a bad influence. Many parents assume that a teen who is socializing with the basketball team, the debating club, the high school yearbook staff, and the high school band is a stable, active, socially happy teen. Teens say this is not necessarily so.

Many teens who contemplate suicide manage a facade of activities that mask their difficulties. They may drift through all the above activities without really talking to anyone in those groups. They may have standards of perfection they can't possibly achieve and, in spite of achievements, constantly feel like a failure. This contributes to their low self-esteem and, despite all that parents would assume to the contrary, they may be unhappy and depressed.

It is not so much what teens' activities are as how they feel about themselves that is significant, and whether they can talk about those feelings to anyone. Try to assess your teen's interaction with friends. Do they listen to each other? Good friends, male and female, consult constantly about many things. They need time to talk.

Parents may feel at a loss to know what is normal teenage behavior and what is a warning sign for suicide. They are often at a loss to know how to deal with a teenager who has grown up in a more democratic society than they did. Is their child undisciplined when he or she disagrees with a parent, or is that healthy independence? Do all teens spend hours in their bedroom listening to rock music on headphones? Or is your teen different?

It is possible to gain a greater understanding of your teen by assessing his or her actions and the actions of the rest of the family. It helps to look at what is happening in your family and what is happening in your teen's life. What behavior worries you?

Worksheet #1 will help you focus on the problems that may need attention in your family.

WORKSHEET #1
ASSESSING YOUR ATTITUDES TO SUICIDE

This worksheet is designed to help you focus on the attitudes in your family that may be making suicide a more likely choice for your teen.

A. Parents' Beliefs

Do you think —

1. that your teen only cares about his/her friends, not about his/her parents?
2. that there is nothing you can do to change your relationship with your teen?
3. that your teen's feelings of incompetence and inadequacy are "normal" and insignificant?
4. that your teen's preoccupation with suicide is an overdramatization of his/her problems?
5. that your teen isn't *really* suicidal, but just talks that way?

Those who answer "yes" to the above may be denying the threat of suicide while withdrawing from involvement with their teen. Where the above attitudes exist it is difficult for teens to talk to their parents about suicide.

B. Barriers to Assessing Your Teen

The following attitudes make it difficult for you to correctly assess the degree of suicide threat in your family.

Do you think —

1. the tendency to suicide is inherited?
2. all suicidal teens look depressed and morose?
3. suicide occurs only in families with grave problems like alcoholism or sexual abuse?
4. suicidal teens do not want to talk to their parents about suicide?
5. teens want to be emotionally isolated from their families?

All the above are false.

C. History of Loss in Your Family

1. Has anyone in your family committed suicide?
2. If yes, did you talk about it with anyone after the funeral? Did you get any counseling?
3. Has any close friend committed suicide?
4. Has anyone in your family attempted suicide?
5. Has any close friend attempted suicide?
6. Has anyone your teen knows committed suicide?
7. Do you think suicide is likely to occur in your family? If yes, why? If no, why not?

Suicide is more likely in a teen who has experienced loss by suicide in someone he/she cares about or can identify with. If any of the above has occurred in your teen's life, he/she is more vulnerable to suicide than many.

6

HOME HELP

a. WHAT CAN YOU DO AT HOME TO HELP THE SITUATION?

If you've looked at your teen and the way your teen fits into your family, and you've defined some of the problems you are having, you now want to do something about them. It sometimes seems that if you could just change his grades, change his friends, give him ambition, drive, courtesy — then all would be well.

But the only person you can change is yourself. You have no power to make changes in anyone else, even in your children. Sometimes changes will occur in other people in the family as they react to the new you, but the only person you can *count* on changing is yourself.

b. HOW DO PARENTS FEEL?

It is often difficult for parents to know how they feel about the child who was once such an understandable personality but who has grown into a stranger. It is difficult to change our behavior if we don't understand the feelings that motivate us. By assessing our families and ourselves we become more aware of what we do and learn to understand how we affect others within the family. We understand better why we act the way we do. We act that way because, in some way, we need to.

If you constantly criticize your teen, it is difficult to stop. The effect of your constant criticism is, as I said earlier, severe. The teen feels rejected and unacceptable.

You may criticize your teen because you believe —

(a) she will remain with you if you continually treat her like a child.

(b) she will need you to guide her always, and you see no other role for a mother or father but one of authority and guidance.

(c) she will listen to you and remain safe from the troubles of the world.

(d) she will listen to you and avoid failure.

(e) it seems less risky to you to take out your anger and frustration (about your job or your marriage) on your child than on your husband/wife/boss.

Or none of the above. These are common reasons parents criticize, but not the only reasons. Your motivation for constantly criticizing your teen results in some kind of satisfaction for you, or you would not do it.

1. How do you feel about your teen?

It is common for parents to tell psychologists, teachers, and the neighbors that the reason they can't deal with their teenager is because she is lazy, selfish, useless, or has some other bad character fault, and that if she just faced up to that fact everything would get better. It is hard for parents to admit that they don't always like their teenager.

Once they do admit this, it is very common for parents to say they can't deal with their teen because he or she is unlovable, lazy, or selfish. This isn't rare. Many parents blame their teens for the mutual dislike. "If he'd just go to school, I could like him." "If she'd just get a job, I'd like her."

The worst aspect of this situation is that teens believe the parents are setting up impossible goals that they cannot achieve and that it is all only an excuse: that no matter what they do, their parents will hate them because, fundamentally, they are no good. Once teens accept their parents' assessment of "no good," then they feel they don't deserve life and happiness.

2. Can you listen?

Teens told me that at the time they tried suicide they felt they could not talk about their feelings to anyone. They felt there was no one who would listen, no one who cared. They said all they wanted was someone to listen uncritically and unjudgmentally, with a caring attitude. That's all.

This does not seem an impossible request, but I understand why it is difficult for parents to fulfill it. Parents feel obliged to do something about information received. It is hard, often impossible, for a parents to hear their teen's problems without immediately offering advice, direction, admonitions, censure, sympathy, comfort, and a plan for change. It is extremely hard just to listen.

One 18-year-old girl told me how she failed to get her parents to listen to her the first time she tried to kill herself.

"I bandaged everything up and my dad, he's Dutch and he's disciplined and dominating, he comes in and says, 'What did you do?' My mom's crying, having the screaming meemies. He said, 'What did you do?' I told him and he said, 'Show me.' And I showed him, and he said, 'Not good enough!' I always remember that. He walked off and said, 'If you wanted to kill yourself, you would have done a better job.'"

While you might be able to defend the father's logic, it would be hard to defend his lack of compassion. It could well be that the father in this instance was trying to convince himself that his daughter did not want to die because *he* didn't want her to die. Perhaps he did love her and perhaps he could not face the idea that she wanted to die. But his daughter was convinced that he despised her because she had failed in a suicide attempt and that she should complete it the next time she tried.

3. Do you understand your teen's view of rejection?

Not all teens who are rejected by their parents will commit suicide. Some will leave home, throw themselves into a career, or join a cult where they feel accepted. But most teens who commit suicide feel rejected by their parents.

Parents often do not believe they reject their teen. They love their child. Most parents would say they love their teen even if they don't approve of him, don't want him around, and constantly criticize him.

It is possible to feel responsible for your teen, worry about her, financially support her, and still reject her. Rejection is obvious to teens. They understand it instinctively and usually assess it accurately. It is less obvious to parents. We prefer not to admit to it and have ways of denying such feelings to ourselves. It is not the parent's view of emotional support, love, and understanding that is important here. It is the teen's perspective that matters. It is their understanding of rejection that affects them. If they feel rejected, not accepted, they suffer — whatever the parent's true feelings are.

A forgiving 20-year-old girl told me, "When I tried suicide last time, the reasons were different from the reasons I had the first time. Last time I was severely depressed and I felt I had nobody. There was nobody there. My parents didn't give me what I needed. It wasn't that they weren't trying; it was that they didn't know how. They didn't know what I was going through."

That statement worried me because either this young woman was denying that her parents were indifferent or her parents, in spite of trying, could not understand her despair.

And how are parents supposed to understand teens' despair? We aren't magically transformed into capable, empathetic psychologists when our children become teens.

Teens do feel isolated from their parents. An 18-year-old told me, "My parents never take time to do things with me. My dad works about 16 hours a day, eats dinner, goes to his bedroom. My mother, she used to be a lot better, but in the last year, she's started doing the same thing. She works for a long time, comes home, makes dinner, goes into the bedroom with my dad. They sit there and watch T.V. They sit there in one world, and I'm in another."

Teens need to be able to talk to someone. Over and over they told me they just needed one person to talk to. That didn't have to be a parent, although they thought being able to talk to a parent was the ideal situation.

Teresa said, "Friends of mine say they did it [tried suicide] because their parents wouldn't listen. Nobody would listen to them. Maybe we're going through typical teenaged problems but it hits some people more severely than some parents think. Parents don't see it. It's like parents think those problems are normal. Well, they're not normal. Problems can get pretty heavy. Especially with the kind of people you get mixed up with. On more than one occasion I've been in over my head and nobody's been there to help me out. Some kids say, 'Oh, I can go to my mom.' Ten to one they couldn't if they really needed her. I bet they couldn't.

"I would have loved to sit and talk to my mother and tell her what was going on. But I was so afraid because of the reactions I'd got before. I mean I'd like to have told her, 'Look, Mom, sex is getting to be a problem for me. I don't know what's right for me.' But if I even mentioned the word, she would have freaked."

Teens judge the degree of rejection not only by what parents say, but by their attitudes and actions. It is necessary to make those attitudes and actions supportive ones.

c. CHANGING YOUR HABITS

You may criticize your teen, then think *after*, "I should not have said [or done] that." That is the first stage of change. Within a short time you will think, "I should not say or do that" *before* you say it. I probably have a permanent groove in my tongue where I've bitten it trying to stop myself from giving advice to my children. For some of us, it isn't easy.

You may find it difficult to change your behavior pattern. Sometimes it may seem that your brain and your mouth are not connected. Your mind tells you not to criticize at the same time you hear yourself doing it.

Most of us are complex people who may have deep needs and motivations for the way we act, and we don't find it easy to change. It is enough to know that whatever the reasons for our actions and attitudes, they affect our teens profoundly.

Teens' problems often come at a time when parents are preoccupied with a great many difficulties of their own — mortgages, educational funds, dentist bills, clothing bills, marriages that are changing, aging parents, and worries over their contribution to life, their expectations for their own fulfillment, and their lack of accomplishments. Parents may need counseling themselves in order to deal with their own overwhelming problems. It may be that they can't work on improving relationships with their teen until they have done this. Very often teens are a casualty of parents' problems, and they can't begin to improve their self-image until parents deal with other family problems.

It is probable that the possibility of teenage suicide is not the only problem in the family, but it is the one that needs immediate attention. In your efforts to understand why *your* teen might choose suicide, it helps to understand what actions of *yours* might be contributing to that choice.

1. Time

Teenagers take time. That can come as quite a shock. Many parents think teenagers live away from home most of the time, at friends' places, at the movies, at school, at school clubs, and in front of their homework. In fact, they can take hours out of your day. Teens need to talk. If you spend half an hour a day listening to your teen, and you have three teens, that's a lot of time out of most parents' busy schedules.

The most independent teenager needs time to talk, even if it is just to inform you of her plans. An independent person is never completely emotionally independent; everyone needs to feel supported and accepted and is never completely independent of a need for others. The better your teens feel about themselves the more independent they are, but they still need time to talk to you.

Making that time can be one of the hardest aspects of living with teenagers. The problem is that teens need parental listening time according to the crises in their lives. They may need two hours of listening time on Monday and then none until Thursday. The fact that you may have a deadline on Monday night, as well as two meetings to attend is often irrelevant. The teen crisis won't wait.

The constant shifting of priorities can be hard to manage. You have to remind yourself that the listening time is vitally important and remember that, like all parents, you may easily underrate the importance of some crises and overrate the importance of others.

2. Listening

It is hard for many parents to listen to their own teens. Parents make wonderful confidants for other people's children. They listen and show encouragement and faith in other people's children but find it hard to listen with that same empathy and faith to their own. Some parents feel that when a teen gives them information about school, sex, or drugs, the parent has to do something about it, that it is the parent's responsibility to —

- intervene in some way in the teen's life, either at school or with their friends,
- give advice on the best way to handle the situation, or
- pass judgment on the rightness or wrongness of the teen's thinking.

Parents need to listen only. That is hard for us to understand. We have spent 15 years or so being responsible parents. Teens need to take responsibility for themselves now. It is time we backed off and listened — although it is very hard not to give an opinion. In fact, teens rarely ask for your opinion. When they don't ask, don't give it. They are far more likely to talk to you and far more likely to ask for your advice in the future if you refrain from giving gratuitous advice. Such advice is usually camouflaged criticism anyway, presented "for his own good." Teens want someone to listen, and they want that someone to be a parent.

I asked the teens I interviewed what they considered the best time of day to talk about the problems that were troubling them. Most said they thought late at night was the best time. Perhaps there is one time of day that seems best for you and your teen.

Listening is not necessarily easy. It ought to be a simple process that requires no thinking, no skill, and no experience. But it is harder to do well than many people suppose. It isn't enough just to listen; you need to convey interest. But many parents convey indifference by the way they listen to their teens. They convey hostility, criticism, even contempt.

Listening, to be beneficial, must be a warm, comfortable process in which your teen feels understood, accepted, and supported. This requires the novice listener to keep in mind some firm rules.

(a) Do not offer advice

If you offer advice you are denying your teen the chance to work out the problem for herself. And you may give the wrong advice since you may not have all the facts. She may not follow your advice and will then be reluctant to talk about the problem again.

(b) Do not criticize, even mildly

There is nothing that stops conversation so completely and so dramatically as criticism.

(c) Do not compare with others

There is always someone better. How would you like to be compared to Tom Sellack or Brooke Shields in looks, or Albert Einstein in intelligence, or Leonardo da Vinci in talent. There is always someone, even close to home, who is more accomplished, more talented, and more hardworking than you are. Your teen may already be suffering from feeling incompetent. He doesn't come to talk to you in order to feel worse.

(d) Do not mitigate or exaggerate the problem

If you tell your teen that the problem isn't as bad as it seems, either he won't believe you or he will feel foolish. It is different for a teen to discover, after talking out a problem, that it isn't as bad as first thought than to be *told* that the problem is minor. Don't exaggerate it either. Your teen will wish he'd never told you if you make too much of it.

(e) Do not sympathize

Many parents think that by offering sympathy to their teen they are offering support. Sympathy is inhibiting. It forces teens to concentrate on how bad they feel, not on the problem. Sympathy is like a blanket thrown over the problem that prevents teens from picking it up and looking at it. There is quite a difference between saying, "That must be hard for you," which shows empathy and respect, and "You poor darling. I don't see how you can manage." The first comment recognizes the difficulty but implies faith in the teen to deal with it. The second comment implies that no one could deal with it.

(f) Express only understanding and acceptance

While this seems very simple when you read it on the page, it is extremely hard to do, especially if you are in the habit of acting differently.

d. WHAT DO YOU WANT?

What kind of a relationship do you want with your teen? You will have some kind of relationship with your teen, whether it is close, distant, mutually caring, or mutually destructive. You may not be able to control what kind of relationship you have — you're not the only one in the relationship and, after all, you can only control your own attitudes and actions. But you may find it helpful to decide what kind of a relationship you truly want.

If you feel that you can't maintain a close relationship with your teen, you need to decide what you *can* manage and how you can ensure that your teen receives the support she needs from someone else, if not from you. If you can't listen, if you find you become too angry, too frustrated, if you cannot resist giving directions or criticizing, enlist the help of a friend or a relative who *can* listen. Does your teen have grandparents, aunts, uncles, or cousins who are talented listeners? If you cannot help your teen right now, ask someone else to do so.

e. LEARNING FROM YOUR TEEN

Our relationship with our teens changes when our teens get older. Be prepared to learn from them. You are no longer the all-knowing one, the wise one, the omnipotent one. You can't know all there is to know about life as teenagers experience it. Your experience is not sufficient to make you qualified to advise them on their lives. The problems are different today and the solutions often beyond our experience. Teens are in a position to educate us in many areas. This is often difficult for parents to appreciate.

Parents may have relied on their children's belief in their omnipotence to maintain their own self-esteem. The child's emerging, more realistic view of parents as fallible humans who make mistakes and have gaps in their knowledge may be harder for parents to accept than it is for children. You feel less of a person when your teen no longer thinks you are totally wonderful.

f. POWER TRIPS

Some parents have invested years in the process of controlling their children and have no idea how to deal with a child who suddenly will not be controlled. In their efforts to maintain the status quo they devise stronger and stronger methods of trying to maintain control while their children devise more and more ways of evading that control. Discipline may escalate from the occasional slap to physical abuse, or from the occasional heated word to constant belittling.

I was surprised to learn how many parents tried to force their teens into obedience through hitting. All the teens I talked to who had been hit repeatedly (15 of the 30) had reached a time between ages 13 and 18 when they refused to take physical abuse any more, and they either hit back or threatened court action. They all stopped their parents from hitting them.

Most parents, even parents who are hitting their children, imposing punishments, and yelling and screaming want to help their children. They want them to be happy and productive. Most parents are looking for ways to help their teens and often feel frustrated because nothing seems to work. Most parents would do almost anything to keep their teen safe.

At the very great risk of oversimplifying, I repeat that the best way to help is to listen.

7

PROFESSIONAL HELP

You may have assessed your family situation, looked at your own parenting abilities or lack of abilities, and decided that your family needs help. Like a car that isn't working properly, your family needs skilled attention.

Unlike a car, your family cannot be driven to a counselor and left for repair. It is not possible to transfer the responsibility for change to a professional. Parents can get help with their efforts to change but they can't drive in, have anger replaced by acceptance, criticism replaced by praise, and dictatorial tones replaced by listening skills, and leave a new person with a life-time guarantee. Counselors help; they do not take charge.

a. COMMITMENT

In order to allow counselors to help, parents must commit time and effort to understanding the problems and working them out. I recall one man who thought he was solving his problems with his family by arranging an appointment with a psychiatrist for his wife and son and telling them to fix up the situation. Since the problem centered around the husband and father, that plan was in trouble from the start.

Usually, both parents and the teen are involved in counseling. Sometimes, psychologists like to see members individually for some of the sessions. But more often, the family goes together.

Counseling takes a lot of time. Parents and other family members have to be prepared to take that time. We are so busy trying to get things done that we may not see the benefits of trying to improve our family situation.

Parents need to be prepared for additional emotional disturbances, as many problems are unearthed at counseling sessions. It is often discouraging to find that the first few counseling sessions seem to be causing more problems, unleashing more anger, than anyone dreamed was hidden in the family.

It seems at first that counseling makes the family situation worse — it is really only making it clearer, showing you what is already there.

b. SEARCHING

A friend of mine told me that in her search for help for her teenage son she spent six months going from school to doctor to helping agency trying to find someone to see him. He had been assessed at his high school as needing help. She was willing to pay for help, yet found "everyone in the assessment business and no one in the helping business." She thought people were more interested in fancy tests than they were in the slow, continuous, consistent process of listening and working through problems.

When searching for a good counselor, you are often too needy to have time to choose a helper carefully. Your problems get worse unexpectedly and you are in immediate need of help. You don't have time to comparison shop for a good counselor. It's much like waiting until your car breaks down before taking it to a mechanic. You roll into the service station and hope the mechanic on duty knows his business.

When your family is in trouble you may sink into the office of the first psychologist you find without any idea if he or she is going to be helpful. Sometimes you just have to take a chance. It is better if you can comparison shop with references from the crisis center, your doctor, the family service center, or from friends.

1. Where to look

Very often, parents finally decide that they must see a counselor only to discover that all available help is booked for six to eight weeks. Free counselors or paid-by-donation clinics are not the only ones to book months ahead. Private psychologists and psychiatrists also book ahead.

For an instant response to a request for assistance parents may find a talking session with a crisis center worker the only available source.

Here are some places to start looking when you decide you need some help:

- a school counselor
- the counseling psychology department of a local university

- your provincial or state registry for psychologists
- the telephone book under counselors, psychologists, family counselors, marriage and family counselors, human relations consultants, and social workers

2. The crisis center

One of the best referral agencies is the local crisis center. A crisis center is readily available (the number is on the inside cover of the telephone book or available from the operator), and can be reached by telephone from almost anywhere. A crisis worker will have a list of publicly funded family counselors and psychologists in your area or can help you find such a list.

Almost all crisis center workers are good counselors. They spend all day listening to people, and they have training in exactly how to do that well. A crisis worker can give you a lot of help on the telephone listening to your problems, to your ideas for solutions, and to your difficulties in getting help. Even the process of explaining your problems may help you to see them more clearly. The workers should be able to give you names, telephone numbers, and even recommendations for good counselors. They can also provide the encouragement you need to persevere in your search.

3. Doctors

Parents often ask their doctors for help with their teens. Doctors, usually general practitioners who must know something about almost everything, suggest counseling, but they may not know which counselor is good with teenagers. There are many counselors who are not. Doctors usually don't have the time to counsel families, and they very often are not skilled at it.

Several teens I interviewed had talked to their family doctors and had not been helped. They received such advice as "You're hurting your parents. Smarten up," and "How could you be so stupid." Such advice only prevented the teens from confiding in the doctors the next time they needed help. The parents of these teens no doubt thought they were helping by sending their teens to the doctor. Be aware that your doctor may not be the one to help your teen.

Having said that, let me hasten to add that there are doctors who do help. Doctors may refer patients to psychiatrists, M.D.s with specialized study, instead of to psychologists who are university trained in psychology with no medical degree.

Psychiatrists are not necessarily better than psychologists, but they are very often covered by a medical plan when psychologists aren't. Psychiatrists can prescribe drugs; psychologists cannot. Psychiatrists seem to be doctors who treat disease while psychologists are counselors who listen. Psychiatrists may not be able to spend as much time with a patient as psychologists can. As with all professionals, the degree of competence and ability to help your family depends on the individual you choose more than on the profession he or she represents.

4. Group counselors

Some crisis centers have parent education groups, or they may participate in parent education groups run by other agencies. For some parents, a group situation is a reassuring reminder that other perfectly normal parents have similar problems. For others, a group situation can be an intimidating and embarrassing statement of failure.

5. School counselors

The school counselor is a busy, overworked individual whose job description may include tailoring classes to suit students; policing tardy students; assisting students who want to drop, change, or add classes; giving in-service education to staff; arranging health films, guidance classes, and visiting lectures; and counseling students who have emotional problems.

While the job description does suggest that they listen to students, the practical challenges of the job often leave little time for this. School counselors rarely have medical or psychiatric support or regular conferences with psychiatrists or psychologists who can give advice on student problems.

Parents who go to school counselors are often reluctant to discuss their teen's problems because they see a counselor as a teacher in a school setting. When parents enter a school building, even as old as they are, they can still be reminded of the "them versus us" atmosphere of the classroom and be reluctant to betray their children's weaknesses to the teacher.

Most often, counselors do not have time to effectively counsel parents anyway and restrict the parent meeting to an effort to deal with behavior problems, grades, or attitudes at school.

6. Mental health counselors

Mental health counselors are available at family service clinics, state or provincial mental health centers, health units, and sometimes private clinics. Mental health counselors can be nurses, social workers, psychologists, or sometimes trained workers under the supervision of nurses or psychologists. They are usually ready to provide long-term counseling and often have practical experience in adolescent counseling. One counselor is not typical of all counselors. If you get a good one, great, but not all counselors are good. If you get a poor one, try to remember that not all counselors are poor and keep looking. It may take time to find someone your family trusts.

Mental health clinics may offer group counseling or group support meetings for teens and parents, or just for parents. A counselor is a member of the group and facilitates discussion and understanding. These groups may be for parents who are having difficulty with their family relationships in general, are having difficulty with alcohol in the family, or are concerned about impending suicide. Groups are often set up to focus on a specific problem.

As with all helping groups and agencies, there are some that are not good. A friend of mine took her daughter to a city-run helping group. The organizers of the group played "Dungeons and Dragons" all through the sessions. There are people like that out there. On the other hand, another friend sat with a psychologist who gave her one suggestion that suddenly made her situation clear and acceptable. It is that kind of help that keeps us looking for a good counselor.

7. Religious counselors

Religious organizations may offer family counseling or group counseling. Many religious counseling services do not restrict their counseling to their own members but are willing to counsel anyone in need. Counselors may be ministers, priests, or rabbis who have some training in counseling or professional psychologists or family counselors hired by the church.

8. Community health nurses

Community health nurses are available to anyone in most areas. Again, their talents and backgrounds differ. Some are excellent listeners while others are not. Community health nurses should be able to refer parents to appropriate counselors and be able to give them some idea of the costs of different services.

9. Social workers

Social workers may be good counselors in some agencies, but generally state and provincial social workers are overworked and crisis-oriented. They respond to emergencies and are not able to give time to preventive measures. Like school counselors, their job description may include doing mountains of paperwork; applying for medical care, funding, housing and social assistance; handling daily telephone calls from schools, hospitals, doctor's offices, health units, and every other social organization in town; and filling out inter-office forms that justify the existence of the social agency to government funding bodies. This leaves little time for listening.

c. WHY PARENTS DON'T GO TO COUNSELORS

Parents may be reluctant to see a counselor because they are unfamiliar with counseling. They have never visited a counselor before and are unsure of how they should act, what they should say, how much they should pay.

Some parents think that talking about intimate family matters with a stranger is dangerous, may be reported to authorities, and is a betrayal of their family. They may be afraid that the counselor will tell them to do things they can't. For instance, a father may be afraid the psychologist will suggest he tell his son he loves him, when he can't even say a civil good morning right now and never tells anyone he loves him or her and isn't even sure if he *does* love his son.

Parents may feel that they will be forced into an awkward, unfamiliar stance that will rob them of dignity and any shreds of control that they have been able to maintain. They may feel that attending counseling sessions is a public admission of failure as a parent. One spouse may feel that a counselor is a friend or ally of the other spouse and that they will gang up and try to make him or her behave a certain way.

If the parents have talked over the problem of the family thoroughly before they seek counseling, it is much easier to make the initial appointment. Usually, though, parents use the counselor to force the problem into the open because they are not able to deal with it, at first, without a counselor.

Once you do find a counselor who is helpful to your family, the sessions should give you a tremendous sense of progress. Your teen should feel that you care enough to make great efforts to help, and your family should feel closer, more supportive, and generally stronger.

This takes time. Having regular sessions with a counselor implies that the family will move along a path of progress. Even booking the next appointment seems a positive step. A counselor holds up a mirror to the family and allows you to see how it works.

Once you understand how the family operates, you have a much better chance of improving the dynamics — and a much better chance of helping your teen. Worksheet #2 will help you focus on what help is available in your community.

WORKSHEET #2
ASSESSING PROFESSIONAL HELP

A. Do you know what emergency help is available in your area?

   1.   Ambulance

      _____

   2.   Crisis center

      _____

   3.   Hospital emergency room

      _____

   4.   Hospital psychiatric assessment and consultation

      _____

   5.   Hospital social worker

      _____

   6.   Family physician referral

      _____

B. Non-emergency help

   1.   Have you called the local crisis center for advice on which counselors are recommended in your area?

   2.   List people you have talked to about your problem including:

      Name _____

      Qualifications _____

      Experience with teenagers and suicide _____

      _____

      Availability

        • appointment within _____ days of calling

        • available on the phone in emergency for consultation?

      _____

      Recommended by _____

Effectiveness
- did the person help?

_____

- did he or she give you ideas that helped?

_____

- did he or she make a difference to your teen's life?

_____

3. How much time per week have you spent with a counselor?

_____

4. How much time do you anticipate spending with a counselor?

_____

5. How much money will you spend trying to get help for this problem?

_____

8

TEEN HELP

a. THE TEEN'S NEED FOR FRIENDS

Teens need friends. That seems a simple, almost self-evident statement, but parents don't always know that. Teens need friends in order to feel accepted, important, and real. As adults do, teens often need time to develop friendships, time to meet, do things together, talk, and trust each other. They must have, somewhere in their schedule, time for friends.

Assess your teen's friends remembering that they are people, not stereotypes. The shaggy, unshaven, ragged clothed, silent teen your daughter brings home may have qualities he is keeping hidden from you but allowing his friends to see.

I managed to get past my own prejudices and the unkempt appearance of one of my son's friends to find a stock-market whiz. It was not that I ignored the two-day old beard and the black leather jacket; it was just that I accepted that he came in a package including black leather jacket (with fringe) and a phenomenal knowledge of the stock market.

Many teens have a carefully constructed facade to effectively keep most adults from knowing them. Deal with your own prejudices. Admit that you have some, and then accept your teen's friends for what they are and what they may allow you to see.

Do not hug your prejudices close with the justification that you are right and that the teens are all wrong and should change to fit what you think are proper conventions. Break through that and try to like your teen's friends. Do not make your teen choose between family and friends. Teens will choose friends.

b. THE SOCIAL GROUP

When teens have low self-esteem, they tend to gravitate to other teens with low self-esteem. This is hard for parents to accept or understand. What is your lovely daughter doing associating with those losers? She is getting something from it; that's what she's doing. She needs something from them. She avoids ridicule from other peers by being assimilated into a small group. She has someone to talk to at class break, at noon. Someone to phone in the evening.

If she has low self-esteem, she has high dependency needs. She has to have friends who include her in their lives. She thinks she is worthless and she desperately wants to be loved. She seeks affection from her peers with such an intensity that peers are often threatened and withdraw, rejecting her. This drives her into further loneliness or into relationships with peers who themselves have such desperate emotional needs for acceptance that they accept bizarre behavior in others.

The problem with the relationships in these groups is that the needs of the individuals are so great that the members of the group are usually unable to help their friends until their own needs are met. A teen in this group may experience superficial acceptance, but basic indifference. In such a situation, a teen's cry of "I'm going to try suicide," may meet with "Go for it. Life's the pits anyway," instead of concern. But even with the inadequacies, the group is of vital importance to the teen. Without this group the teen is even more lonely, more isolated, more withdrawn.

Sometimes teens will deliberately seek situations that reaffirm their low social standing. Because they feel worthless they look for social situations that prove they are worthless.

A teen with low self-esteem may also feel that anything he does is doomed to failure, that any social effort he makes will fail. Therefore, he might as well seek what in his opinion is the lowest social situation he knows. That way, failure to assimilate into this group will not be as traumatic as failure with a desirable and admired group. He isn't risking as much, so he won't lose as much.

Don't cut off sources of friendship as a punishment. When teens are in trouble they need their friends more than ever. If they didn't need those friends on some level, they would not be associating with them.

c. WHAT CAN YOU DO TO FURTHER TEENS' FRIENDSHIPS?

To start with, do not criticize your teen's friends. They, at least, are friends and your teen needs them. Find something to like about them. Treat them as valued people. Take time. Be willing to learn from them. Make opportunities to get to know your teen's friends. Include one on an outing such as swimming, skiing, or fishing. It is hard to include a teen you don't approve of. But if you can, the experience can give you a greater understanding of your own child.

Learn something new with your teen and his friends — curling, how to tie flies, how to make chocolates. Allow yourself to be vulnerable. Make mistakes along with your teens so they and their friends know you are not perfect. Therefore, they don't have to be perfect; there is room in their lives for mistakes.

Learn to listen to teens in a group. If they are defensive, change your approach. Perhaps you are condescending, flippant, over-talkative because you feel inept. Try to show acceptance, interest, and concern. If you are on a friendly basis with them you can, at a time when you are worried about your son, ask his friends if they know of anything you can do that will help. This means you have to have a background of friendly relations then in order to get their advice.

Their advice might be of great value — something you hadn't thought of, didn't know was worrying your son, or had no idea was influencing his life. Your teen's friends have to trust you. Trust takes time and involvement. They will not admit you into their group as an equal, but they may be friendly.

d. WHAT TO SAY TO YOUR TEEN'S FRIENDS

State the obvious with teens —

- Yes, I like you.
- Yes, I think you are a nice guy.
- Yes, I think you have enough brains to survive in the world.
- Yes, I think you are managing better than I did as a teen.

They need to hear something sincerely positive every day.

e. DO TEENS KNOW THE COMMUNITY HELPERS?

Does your teen and her friends know the people in your community who can help? Are there teen counselors at school, in the community, at the drop-in center? Does your teen know the crisis center number? Do her friends know the crisis center number? Do they know the name of an adult counselor they can go to for help? Is there a youth line in your community at the crisis center?

What helping groups are available at the crisis center, school, church, mental health clinic? Are the services free? (The fear of having to pay for services keeps teens away from them.)

f. HOW CAN YOUR TEEN MAKE MORE FRIENDS?

What opportunities does your teen have for making more friends in social groups in the community, at church, school, camps, on ski trips, swimming meets, by hanging around the mall, the pool hall, the bowling lanes, the beach, the neighborhood house?

Stop looking at your teen's behavior as bad, morally wrong, or even criminal. Look at it as temporary and symptomatic of a problem. Life would not be suddenly wonderful if your teen stopped arguing with you; you would just not know about his problems.

Many parents recognize that in their desire to have certain behaviors stop, they are really hoping that the underlying problem that causes the behavior will go away. If the behavior stopped, but the anxiety was still there, the teen would no doubt show his anxieties in other ways. If your teen's problem is low self-esteem and he stops hanging around with the riff-raff, he may just become more lonely, more withdrawn, and more suicidal.

You do not need to fix the behaviors, you need to understand them. You need to know why your teen needs these behaviors. Why does she need to go to the rock concert? To feel part of a group? What can you do to help her need for peer acceptance if you don't want your 13-year-old to go to the rock concert?

Perhaps you can only express your understanding of such a need. Perhaps you can't make everything work out for her. But you can't be indifferent to her needs. You can't let her think that you don't care. Indifference translates into hate in the minds of teens. If you are indifferent, she knows she is unworthy of anyone's admiration or love. She feels she's useless, worthless, and she might as well be dead.

g. WHAT DO TEENS WANT FROM THEIR FRIENDS?

Parents want productivity, compliance, and control. Teens want acceptance, understanding, and support. Teens look to their friends for the acceptance they need and must have. This is in no way a substitute for parental approval. In fact, if parental approval is lacking, teens find it difficult to get enough support from friends.

Friends should expand and develop the basic feeling of worth that teens get from their supporting and accepting parents. When this parental support is lacking, teens search desperately for others who can make them feel worthwhile. They then put unrealistic demands on their friends for support and encouragement, and very often the friends can't sustain such a role.

When friends fail a teen, she is convinced again that she is worthless. There seems to be a basic belief among teens that if your parents don't love you, no one can. But they try to create a network of friends that will support them. Some do succeed. Many don't.

Worksheet #3 at the end of this chapter will help you evaluate your teen's chances of getting help from his or her friends.

h. WHAT IS INDEPENDENCE?

It seems that parents are asked to allow their children to make independent decisions and at the same time stay involved with and supportive of them. This is not such a contradiction as it seems. We are involved with our own friends, yet don't make their decisions for them. We are often involved with our brothers and sisters, but don't take on their obligations or responsibilities.

It is an act of faith to allow our teenagers to make their own decisions. We must let them fail, make mistakes, make the wrong decisions, while at the same time show them we accept and support them. We need to look at the D in math and show that we understand that this is a problem for the teen. We don't tell her what she must do about it. We don't tell her how to study. We listen. We don't offer solutions. It is her math mark.

If that seems too uninvolved, too vague, consider what happens if you do become involved. If you take responsibility for your daughter's math mark and outline a course of studies she must follow, from 7:00 to 9:00 every night, then you must police such a course. This will affect your relationship every day. You are the police, she is the policed. She isn't handling the problem herself, you are.

If you listen to her without offering advice, you may find that the low math mark stems from reasons you would never have considered. The math class is at 8:15 every morning and she never makes it. She is taking calculus and she doesn't understand it. Her math teacher is sexually harassing her.

When you simply listen, you have a much greater chance of truly helping your daughter explore the causes of her problem, and from there, helping her solve it. Until she sees the problem, she won't see the solution. And you can't impose it.

Often, especially if communication has not been good, a teen may tell a parent, "Nothing's wrong. I just got a lousy grade." It is enough to express your concern that he is having trouble. That is enough. If he doesn't want to tell you, he won't. Wait. Express faith in his abilities to deal with his own problems and wait.

We must stop directing, punishing, and rewarding. We need to relinquish that kind of control over teens' lives. It is difficult if we have found such methods to be effective when they were younger, but we are raising children to make their own decisions and we must let them practice. It's our job to listen and try to understand life from their point of view. Their lives are different from ours. Their decisions must be theirs alone.

i. USING RELIGION

Some parents use religion as a means of controlling their teens. They tell themselves they are only protecting their child from the dangers of the world as they impose rigid rules of conduct. They try to push their ideas, ambitions, or morals onto their teens. Teens must accept ideas, ambitions, and morals in their own time, at their own rate, in their own way.

You can't use threats to get compliance with your rules and the rules of your religion without paying a huge price for it in severed communication and withdrawal.

You can expose your teens to your religion and hope that they will use the recipe you have found useful to guide your own life, but when you use your religion to back up your authority, you run the very great risk that your teen will reject your religion along with your authority. They know you are using religion as a whip in an effort to control their lives.

Do you want your teen to develop spiritually? Or do you want your teen to adopt your religion so that you can be assured that he will respond to your authority? Question your motives. If you are using your religion to add authority to your own words, then you are in danger of forcing your teens to repudiate religion as they attain an independent life.

If you allow your teens the freedom of exploration, they may find peers and mentors within your religious community that will help them. A religious community is an excellent place for teens to find friends and adult counselors. However, too much pressure to comply with rules and regulations will prevent this. Your teens' experience with that religious community is theirs alone, and they must develop it as they decide. Allow them that opportunity.

j. HOW CAN TEENS HELP?

Because teens need friends they will seek them out. How helpful friends will be depends on the maturity, abilities, and concerns of those friends. Since most teens are more likely to talk to their friends than to their parents or any other adult, it is important that those friends be alert to the possibilities of suicide and knowledgeable about how to deal with such signs.

While parents are unlikely to be effective in interfering with friendships or instructing such friends, it is possible to make a difference in your community by making sure that suicide risk factors are posted in the schools or handed out in guidance or health classes, that the telephone numbers of the crisis centers are on the bulletin boards at the schools and other teen gathering places such as malls or theaters.

Parents can ask at the beginning of the school term what plans the school has to provide suicide education. Parents can leave books or brochures on suicide prevention around the house, or give them to their teens and their friends. They can see that the school library and the public library have a display of such books or pamphlets.

Parents can provide the social services agencies (police, public health nurses, social workers) with the numbers of crisis intervention agencies and with brochures and pamphlets on suicide prevention. All these activities should result in an increased awareness in teens of their responsibilities to each other when one of them is suicidal.

You can be the adult friend to your child's friends. They may not talk to their own parents, but they might talk to you. That means you have to take time to get to know them. That means you have to be non-judgmental. And it means you have to deal with your own prejudices — that you can't just withdraw and wait until your teen grows up and past "all this trouble." He might not live that long.

WORKSHEET #3
ASSESSING TEEN HELP

1. How much help is available to your teen through his/her friends?
    _____
    _____

2. Does your teen have a friend who is a confidant, someone he/she can tell his/her feelings to? True friends who are reliable and receptive take time to make. A teen who has recently moved or frequently moves is less likely to have a network of supporting friends than one who has kept the same circle of friends for years.
    _____
    _____

3. Does your teen have time to talk to his/her friends? Does his daily schedule (school, work, family, church) leave time for him to talk to his/her friends?
    _____
    _____

4. Do your teen's friends know much about suicide? _____
    Do they know who is likely to try suicide? _____
    Do they know where to get adult help? _____
    Do they know where to get emergency treatment? _____
    Do they know where to get counseling? _____

5. Do your teen's friends visit in your house? _____
    Do they talk in front of the adults in your house? _____
    Do they visit in the house of his/her friends? _____
    Do they have an adult friend? _____
    Who is their adult friend? _____
    Can they get help from this friend if they are worried about suicide? _____

6. Do your teen's friends care enough about him/her to try to prevent his/her suicide?
    _____
    _____

9

HOW DO YOU RAISE A CHILD
TO AVOID SUICIDE?

a. FEELING ACCEPTED

We want to do all we can to keep our teens healthy and to promote their long life. Just as we try to immunize against disease, so would we like to immunize against suicide. There is no guarantee that any child will not try suicide, but there are some attitudes that create a family climate that makes suicide a less likely choice for teens. They are less likely to try suicide if —

(a) they live in a family atmosphere of pleasurable acceptance,

(b) they believe their parents like them and are glad they are part of the family,

(c) someone listens to them, and

(d) they feel confident and capable of dealing with the problems that come up in their lives.

b. TEACHING TEENS TO DEAL WITH STRESS

One way to train your child to avoid the choice of suicide is to teach him or her how to deal with stress. Because so much of what you teach is taught by example, you must examine how you deal with stress. Do you react to stress with music, aerobic workouts, swimming, alcohol, television, sex, housecleaning binges, rages?

You need to have some idea of how you view stress in your own life. Do you think it is bad? Harmful? Do you think it will overwhelm you if you don't take steps to avoid it? Or do you see stress as part of your day, a part that you are sure you can deal with. If you see stress as an ogre ready to pounce, your teen will probably be anxious about it. If you see stress as normal, and yourself as capable of dealing with it, your teen will probably absorb that also.

A hard day at the office may deserve a comment and a demonstration of your ability to relax over dinner or in front of the television. If a hard day at the office means you have to hit the bars all weekend in order to be able to cope on Monday, you have a problem with stress.

Because parents aren't perfect, it may be that the best you can do for your teen is to talk about your difficulties with stress. Try to show him that there are other ways of dealing with it, that you hope he will learn better ways.

c. TEACHING TEENS TO DEAL WITH PAIN

Part of our North American culture over the last 30 years has included an attempt to avoid any kind of pain. If you have a headache, you must have a headache pill. If you have a cut, you need a bandage. If you have an ache in a muscle, you need to have it rubbed. We have been teaching our children that no one has to have pain.

We have taken it further and told them that happiness is the norm, that no one should be unhappy and that unhappiness should be "fixed." A steady, subtle pressure is exerted on this generation of teens to be happy and pain-free at all times. Anything less is not normal.

Parents have supported this attitude by being quick to apply the bandage and to administer the headache pill. Rarely do parents of elementary school children expect their children to be able to deal with the pain of a scraped knee or bruised elbow. In general, parents are more anxious to make the hurt go away than to support the child's method of dealing with it.

When, as a nurse, I gave immunization shots, I explained to nervous kindergarten children, "Yes, it will hurt a little as the medication goes in, but if you take a deep breath and let it out slowly when I tell you, you can deal with it." They seldom panicked.

These five-year-old children knew an adult expected them to look after themselves, that she was sure they could, and they did. By actively handling their own fears and their own pain they had more confidence to face the next fear, the next pain.

Pain is a part of life. Dealing with pain is part of living. We know that, but we don't make that clear to our children. I'm not talking of the severe pain of a broken hip or a burn — pain in those cases is overwhelming — but the everyday pains of ordinary life.

If we teach children to deal with pain by escaping in drugs ("Have a headache pill"), in denial ("This won't hurt a bit"), and in avoidance ("Don't go to the party if you are embarrassed"), we do not equip them with the ability that they need as teens to deal with pain.

In the small pains and disappointments of elementary school, children learn confidence in their ability to handle problems. If they haven't learned this, they have learned other ways of dealing with problems — with escape, denial, and avoidance. As much as we try to protect children from frightening or painful situations, they do meet them and they need to be taught how to meet them.

Elementary school children trust their parents' advice. If you tell them that it helps to take a deep breath and count to five before they tackle a problem, they will try it. If you tell them to try to think of two choices as solutions to a problem, they will try it. Then they will feel that they *are* handling their own problems. Such small beginnings build great confidence.

The concept that all pain demands relief, that any pain requires a drug, makes the transfer from headache tablets to other drugs easy. The teen is conditioned to look for pain relief.

Emotional pain is very often treated in the early years the same way as physical pain. Parents want their children to be continually happy, forget pain, or pretend they are not hurt. They want them to escape pain, avoid it, or deny it.

Children approach teen life with little experience in dealing with emotional pain. With laudable intentions of protecting their children, parents prevent them from handling humiliation, anger, fear, and frustration. In some ways encouraging children to deny, avoid, or escape pain in the early years trains them to look for the ultimate escape in suicide.

Teens often have the uncomfortable conviction that if they were really competent they would never feel pain. Confessing to the feelings of hurt, anger, and humiliation is impossible for many teens. When they are unable to admit these feelings, they cannot get help in dealing with them.

Children and teens need help in dealing with pain. They don't need someone to take on their pain and magically make it disappear. They need some direction in how to handle it. That means that parents need to examine how they deal with pain, physical and emotional, and what they consider effective and ineffective. Teens often assimilate their parent's methods of coping. If a parent threatens suicide or physical separation, the teen is more likely to see suicide, a permanent separation, as a choice.

It also means that children need continual support and appreciative comments when they handle a difficult problem, even if they don't handle it perfectly. They need to know that their parents appreciate their efforts. It helps children to realize that parents don't always handle all situations perfectly either. They need to hear their parents evaluating a failure. "What I should have done was...." "The next time I'll try...." They need to see that everyone handles problems, some days better than others. They need to feel confident that they can also.

d. TEACHING TEENS TO HANDLE LOSS

If children experience the loss of a relative, a friend, even a pet, parents need to explore that loss with them. Children need help in obtaining faith in their ability to deal with such loss. It is often a series of losses, unresolved, unaccepted, unexplored, that culminate in a suicide attempt. Do not deny the importance of any loss. If your teen will not talk about a loss, at least let him or her know that you think it was important.

e. PROVIDING NETWORKS

While children are going through the elementary grades, it is important to build a network of activities and relationships that can act as a safety net when the burdens of decision and depression fall in the teen years.

Elementary school children are likely to be enthusiastic about new activities. Teens are more likely to be interested only in those activities they can do well. The more activities teens have that interest them, the more people they know, the more competent they feel. Generally, that is. Sometimes this is not true. There are teens who are very accomplished, busy, and active but feel that nothing they do is ever good enough.

Be sure that the interests your children pursue in elementary school are *their* choices so that their interest will continue into the teen years. Activities that were parents' choices in elementary school are unlikely to be pursued into high school except by the "perfect child" who is living out his parents' dreams. Such teens have their own overwhelming pressures, keeping a busy schedule of activities hoping to please their parents, their friends, and themselves.

It is important to allow elementary school children a chance to develop strong long-term relationships with relatives and friends outside the immediate family. If, during the teen years, they feel that their parents do not understand them and make them feel inadequate or incompetent, this network of reliable friends and relatives can give them acceptance and support.

If, as often happens, your child hits the teen years just as you and your spouse hit marital, financial, or career difficulties and you have little time for your teen, they have a back-up extended "family" that can give them a sense of worth. Such friends and relatives are not a substitute for parents, but they may be a life-saving temporary alternative.

f. PLEASING MOM AND DAD

When children are in elementary school they play the game of working for their parents' approval. If their parents' love and acceptance is conditional on achievements, children try very hard to achieve. When they reach the teen years, they feel that the expectations of parents, friends, and teachers are overwhelming, and they stop trying to please. Since their acceptance and support was hinged on achievement, they may suddenly, at a time when they most need it, lack parental support.

g. INCREASING SELF-ESTEEM AND CONFIDENCE

Teen years are the years that parents need to shovel in tons of approval and loving affection. The trouble teens experience at this time never equals the amount of love they receive. As children approach their teen years, parents should increase the amount of support they give at the same time they decrease the amount of authority they exert, so that teens feel that they are capable of handling most problems.

It is not enough to deal with your teen in the same way you dealt with him or her as a child. You must reassess your actions, ideas, and relationships. It may be time for a new beginning.

10

HOW DO YOU LISTEN TO YOUR TEEN?

a. OPPORTUNITIES TO LISTEN

Typically, after you have decided that you *must* be more open to your teenager, you *must* be available to her, you *must* listen to her, she disappears into her school, television, and social life, only stopping periodically in front of the fridge or behind the bathroom door. There never seems to be an opportunity to sit and listen. She doesn't want to talk to you.

If you are having great difficulty, make a date with your teen for lunch at a restaurant, just the two of you. Or make a date for a walk or bowling or some activity that forces the two of you to be together.

If her experience has been that time spent with you leaves her feeling inadequate ("shitty" is the word I've heard most), then she will avoid you since she doesn't trust your intentions. Avoiding you is a reasonable protective attitude. But, in spite of their evasive tactics, teens tell me they want a relationship with their parents. If you make the effort, your daughter will eventually give you a chance.

b. THE AGENDA

When you finally get together, don't expect anything from your teen but her physical presence. You are not having this lunch or walk so that you can make her talk. You are having it so you can give her your attention. If your teen doesn't talk to you, count the event successful if you manage to let her know you like her.

Don't set an agenda for this time together. Don't decide that in this time your teen is going to do anything or say anything, since her speech and activities are not within your control. You are responsible only for your actions and your emotions. Try to make the outing with your teen pleasant — not deep and meaningful — but pleasant. Then repeat it. Your objective is to convince her that you like her as she is.

While you might be able to achieve this at home, there may be too many negative associations with home to make it possible. The home is parental turf where parents have "ruled." Teens evolve habitual reactions in their homes: evasion, resentment, withdrawal. They may find it easier to shed these reactions outside the familial nest.

It is also easier for you to concentrate on your teen when you are out of the home at a restaurant or park where you can't be distracted by other children arriving and departing, the telephone ringing, the dinner boiling over, the office phoning for advice and information.

c.   HABITS OF CONVERSATION

Parents and teens may have developed a discouraging pattern of conversation that is difficult to change. With the best intentions you find yourself asking a question that you swore you were not going to ask. "How's your French mark?" for instance when you know that French is her worst subject. Her reaction, either out of her mouth or in her mind, will probably be, "You ask about my worst subject. You know it's my worst subject. You're telling me I'm stupid." That wasn't your intention. You didn't want her to feel stupid, you just wanted reassurance that she wasn't failing French. She thought you were attacking her. Conversation ceases.

When you are trying to change your non-helpful habits, you will often say something you would love to retract. You recognize it as a mistake as soon as it leaves your mouth. It seems to hang in the air in front of you flashing with neon light. The trick is to learn to recognize comments like that before you say them; then don't say them.

It is easier to change your habits of speech when your attitude to your teen changes. You find that old comments gradually disappear from your conversation as new, positive ones become more habitual. Be forgiving of yourself; change like this takes repeated practice.

d.   GETTING RID OF BARRIERS TO COMMUNICATION

If you have seen yourself as a guide, director, and teacher of your child, it is difficult to accept a more passive supporting role. Acceptance and support are not indifference. You do care about your teen; you are interested. It takes more time and energy than you might expect to be a supporting, non-interfering parent. It also requires a new vocabulary.

You need to delete from your language sentences that begin with:

- You ought to
- Why don't you
- Have you tried
- Most kids your age
- When I was your age
- You need to
- You should
- You must

Those statements expose your mistrust of your teen's ability to cope. You are telling her that she needs your advice, that she can't manage on her own, that she is incompetent. Any statement from you that criticizes, judges, directs, gives solutions, analyzes, and diagnoses her problems or puts her through an interrogation undermines her faith in herself.

She needs you to bolster that faith, not reduce it. She doesn't need you to map out life for her. She needs to discuss her ideas with you but not to take her ideas from you. That is hard for some parents to accept if they are used to being in charge of their child's life. For them, being a parent means being in charge. Some parents have no other area of their lives where they are the authority, and they don't want to give up this one.

1. Name calling

Some parents have fallen into the habit of calling their teen names. Before you leap to your own defense with "not me," consider what you do call your teen. If you say to your teen, "You are lazy," "You are stupid," "You are a failure," "You are reckless," "You are crazy," you are calling her names. You run the great risk of having your teen believe you.

Parents very often don't think they are so powerful in their children's lives that they can label their child and cause him to live up to that label. But, they are, so the teens tell me. Parents tell their teen he is lazy so he will work harder. What happens is that the teen doesn't work harder, he accepts the parents' evaluation and believes that he is lazy. If you, the parent, tell your child he is inadequate, he will believe you. Name-calling is one of the most destructive habits that parents have.

2. Teaching

One adolescent psychologist told me that he considered the worst thing a parent of teens could do, worse than name-calling and worse than physically abusing them, was to lecture. Lecturing, he thought, was harder on teens — more demoralizing, destructive, demeaning — than any other controlling tactic parents used.

You may be able to feel resistance in the air when you start to lecture. It may be easier to notice what happens when your spouse or partner starts to lecture. There is a general stiffening of the atmosphere. In some families, when lecturing starts teens argue. In some they walk away. In some they say nothing but they stop listening. Lecturing is ineffective. It doesn't help your teen at all. We have vast experience at being lectured ourselves but somehow that still doesn't make us aware of how ineffective it is.

3. Praise

It is difficult to understand how praise could possibly hurt a teen, but praise can be manipulative. "Your straight As are absolutely wonderful. Look, neighbor, my daughter has straight As. Isn't she wonderful?" The implication to your daughter is that she is wonderful *only* when she has straight As.

When your teens tell you about their accomplishments, you need to share their sense of achievement without dishing out praise as if their achievement was the only thing you liked about them.

Many parents were exposed to the theory that parents should praise "good" behavior in children and ignore "bad" in order to get children to repeat the good behavior and drop the bad. This was a step up from the spanking for bad behavior that the generation before us practiced. But it is still a method of manipulating and controlling behavior which, however appropriate for young children, is doomed to failure in teens. Teens resent being manipulated, even by praise. And they resist it.

It is one thing to tell your son when he has found the answer to a difficult math problem that he must feel good about that and another to tell him he is always so wonderful at school. He will be very uncomfortable with the second comment. He knows he isn't always wonderful at school and he worries that you might expect more than he can give, or that you expect him to do that well on every test. Teens may feel that parents praise in order to manipulate or at the wrong time, showing that they don't understand their teen's life.

4. Agreeing

Agreeing with your teen isn't always wise either. You can accept the fact that your teen feels a certain way, recognize that she has chosen to deal with a problem one way, give her emotional support for her choice ("That must have been hard to decide, but I think you can deal with it.") without agreeing with that choice. Agreeing is seen by teens in much the same light as praising. Teens may be suspicious that it is manipulative. Supporting, on the other hand, is seen as an emotional plus. Teens realize that you can support their choices without agreeing with them.

e. HOW TO COMMUNICATE

If the above are ways *not* to communicate with your teen, what are ways *to* communicate? It is surprising how little you need to say to convey understanding. Most counselors have a standard group of what I call psychological uhms and hums. "Is that right?" "I see." "Uh huh." "Umm hmm." "Oh." These encouraging noises said with an interested tone of voice can show a great deal of acceptance.

If you are finding it hard to think of something nonjudgmental to say you might keep in mind a few standby comments such as "Tell me about it." (This seems to me to be the most sincere comment you can make. You do want to know the teen's problem, and this comment comes to mind quickly.) Then wait. Silence can show acceptance and support.

The following comments can sometimes be useful. They can also act as barriers to communication if used insincerely or inappropriately.

- "Others feel this way, too."
- "I'm sure you can handle this."
- "I know you are capable."
- "What are you going to do about that?"
- "Are you happy with your decision?"
- "Do you want to talk about it?"
- "This is important to you."
- "I'd like to know how you feel."
- "Your point of view is different from mine, and it's interesting to hear how you feel about things. You're my window into a different age, a different culture."

Be sure that you have the intention of accepting and trying to understand your teen, that your objective in taking time to be with him is not to change him, guide him, or manipulate him (for his own good), but to listen and to understand.

Teens have an incredibly accurate radar for their parents' intentions. They often know what their parents' intentions are when the intentions are obscure to the parents.

f. LETTING GO

When you form the intention of *not* trying to change your teens, just trying to appreciate them and listen to them, it relieves you of a great deal of pressure — although many parents are not comfortable with this. They feel that they should be trying to change their teenagers. It helps if parents determine that, just for this one outing, this one lunch, this one movie date, they will relinquish their role as prime director in their teen's life, and listen.

g. SUPPORTING TEENS

It is amazing to me that our children don't realize how much we care about them. It seems obvious to me that if we feed, cloth, chauffeur, listen to, advise, urge, question, and admonish our teens, they will understand that we love them. But they don't. They need to hear, "You are great. You are a fine daughter. You are a delight."

Many of us are not comfortable with terms of endearment. We think telling a child "I think you are great" is sentimental and unnecessary. It is not. From the teen's point of view, it is essential.

h. MAGICAL REPAIRS TO RELATIONSHIPS

Sometimes it is difficult to persevere in your efforts to reach your teen when you meet rejection. To change a judgmental, critical, adversarial relationship to a helping, supportive one takes time. We cannot go to a counselor once and get "everything fixed." We cannot feed our child a magic vitamin and have him be everything we want in a teen. We cannot send our child to a finishing school and have her come home loving, dutiful, and obedient. This simply won't happen.

Our generation of parents seems to lean to the magical cure of professional counselors. Our generation seems to believe that if you drop your teen off with his problems to a counselor every Friday for a year, he will be fixed. A year's worth of counseling may help your teen, and it may not. It is no substitute for your attention and your support.

i. THE PERFECT TIME TO START LISTENING

There is no perfect time to start listening to your teen. Whenever you start, communication will probably be difficult and feel awkward. One teen I know has a masterful technique of saying absolutely nothing when he doesn't want to talk. This is daunting. It is extremely difficult to hold a conversation with a teen who won't talk. If you attempt to schedule a "heart to heart" conversation with your teen you may run into this silence technique. In that situation it is far easier to have a comfortable time while doing something else, like eating lunch or bowling.

The first few times you try to listen and accept your teen without advising or teaching or judging him, you will find that you slip back into old habits. That's normal. Change takes time and effort. Keep trying.

You can make a difference over time in your relationship with your teen. You can make a difference in his feelings of competence and his perception of his own worth. Teenagers who try suicide usually feel inadequate and unloved. It is vitally important that you show your teen that you have faith in him and that you care. You need to do this continually and consistently.

11

SUICIDE RISK FACTORS, ATTEMPTS, COMPLETION

a. SIGNS AND SYMPTOMS OF IMPENDING SUICIDE

While teens are unique, different from one another in personality and family composition, in life experiences and goals, they often have similar reactions to stress and show similar signs and symptoms of impending suicide. Parents need to be aware of these signs so they can stay alert to the possibility of suicide.

Parents need to realize that many teens think about the possibility of suicide in general terms without seriously considering it for themselves. Teens who are theoretically interested in suicide may talk about it without seeing it as an answer to their problems. Those who do see it as an answer give indications they are considering it.

1. Suicide in the near future

Parents also need to be aware that a teen who has lost a family member to suicide is predisposed to think of suicide as a choice that is acceptable to his family, or to think that suicide is his destiny.

Parents need to be more alert to a teen's problems around his birthdates. Teens tend to try suicide most often in the two weeks following their birthdays. One study reported the likelihood of suicide in this period was three times more than expected.

When planning suicide in the near future, teens often show the following tendencies:

(a) Isolate themselves from others

They may distance themselves by watching television continually, listening to music for hours, daydreaming all the time. They may increase their distancing by refusing to talk or developing monosyllabic speech patterns: "Yes," "No," "I don't know." They sometimes distance and isolate themselves by ridiculing and making sarcastic and vicious remarks about others.

(b) Become preoccupied with death

They talk about death in relation to others, or wars or concepts. They may write poetry that contains allegories about death. They may write English assignments that discuss death. They may buy music and play games that are concerned with death. Sometimes they wear T-shirts that advertise their preoccupation with death.

While some of these symptoms may have been occurring for months, the amount of time the teen spends using these methods of coping increases.

(c) Have an increased number of physical problems or accidents

These may be unconscious bids for help that are more socially acceptable than a suicide attempt. Parents and medical professionals very often miss the teen's underlying feelings.

(d) Get into trouble at school, academically or socially or both

They may start skipping school and are often absent the day before they try suicide.

(e) Have an emotional "deadness"

They manage to exist in the family and at school without being touched emotionally by anyone.

2. Imminent suicide

Parents often react to the above signs and symptoms with frustration and anger. They see their teen as self-indulgent and weak, and they have difficulty seeing behavior like this as symptomatic of suicide. Parents often get used to their teen's behavior and tell themselves, "She's always like this" and discount the importance of such symptoms. But the signs should be taken seriously.

Teens who have tried suicide before are still at risk. Although it would seem reasonable for parents to be alert to a repeated attempt at suicide, some parents do not think that people who have tried suicide before and not died will try it again with the intention of dying. They may. The following are signs that suicide is imminent:

(a) Giving possessions away

Teens will give away small, sentimentally valued items as well as stereos, computers, and clothes.

(b) Making remarks suggestive of suicide

Teens will use phrases such as "ending it all," "getting out," "not being around to bother anyone," "getting rid of all my problems." Remarks like these are often difficult for parents to notice since teens often use extravagant language, "I thought I'd die!" "That's radical." Parents get used to hearing dramatized language and may miss the real despair behind the words.

b. FAMILY PATTERNS

The teen's desire for suicide comes out of his interactions with his family. The families of teens who try suicide often have many traits in common.

There is not a great deal of research on some of these characteristics, but it is thought that certain family patterns are more likely to lead teens to suicidal tendencies than other patterns. Families that contribute to a teen's suicidal tendencies are ones in which —

(a) there is a warm and possessive mother and a distant and hostile father,

(b) the teen is singled out to be the troublemaker, the scapegoat, the expendable one who is not accepted by the family just as he is,

(c) the teen is sometimes thought of as "just like grandpa" or "just like your father" or "just like" someone the family doesn't accept,

(d) the family tries to keep members from seeking intimacy with non-family members,

(e) there are long-term patterns of depression, alcoholism, and drug abuse,

(f) there is anger and communication difficulties between mother and father, or

(g) the family is not flexible. Any change in status, achievements, jobs, earning power, goals is interpreted as threatening the family.

Not all these symptoms necessarily occur in one family, but to the extent that any one of the symptoms of family dysfunction contribute to the teen's feelings of inadequacy and his conviction that he is not accepted by his family, they contribute to his desire for suicide.

c. THE TRIGGER EVENT

Increasing stress can precipitate a teen into suicide, but very often the trigger event is a loss.

The most devastating experience for teens when they are in a state of low self-esteem is a loss. Usually this is a loss that is in addition to other losses that have gone before. The teen experienced an earlier loss — a friend, a parent — and this trigger event is another. It could be the loss of an elective office at school, a canceled band trip, the end of a girlfriend-boyfriend relationship, the loss of a father or mother in separation or divorce.

The loss only has to be important to the teen to be significant. It doesn't have to be understood as loss by anyone else. One girl I talked to was precipitated into a suicide attempt by her graduation from high school. She saw her friend, the high school counselor, as lost to her. And it was more than she could, at that time, deal with.

Teens are unable to see at that time that life will get better. Life consists of right now. They are convinced that there is nothing worth living for. This is not always after being depressed — teens may contemplate suicide without going through a deep depression.

The relationship that exists between parents and teen at the time of the loss is of great importance to the teen's ability to deal with that loss. The less support the teen feels from the parents, the less likely he is to be able to handle loss. One study reported that one-third of suicide attempts occurred after an argument with parents. Teens see the loss of parental support as important.

Some suicide attempts occur at the diagnostic stage of a physical illness. Teens fear the loss of physical competence or beauty as a side effect of the illness or the surgery.

Worksheet #4 can help you evaluate the signs and symptoms of suicide.

d. WHAT YOU CAN DO

1. Evaluate the risk of suicide

You can make every effort to keep your teen safe. This means evaluating the risk of suicide. Usually this means talking it over with someone you trust and someone who knows your teen well.

A suicidal crisis is no time to allow a teen to make choices that will leave him with failure. It isn't the time to allow him to experience failure. Failure in this instance means death. When in a suicidal crisis a teenager is not able to make positive, rational choices. He needs to have protection until he is able to function normally again.

At some time, you will have to "let go" and allow him the room to grow and make decisions, but that is not appropriate during his deep despair and cloudy perspective.

2. Ask your teen whether she is considering suicide

Talk about it. Let her "sound off," relieve her feelings. Those who talk about it to a compassionate listener are far less likely to attempt suicide than those who have no one to talk to. A part of them wants to live. They say, "Listen to me, so I can live."

Most teens are relieved to talk about suicide. It may take them several attempts before they trust anyone enough to talk, but they want to do it, and feel emotionally relieved when they do do it.

This listening requires parents to put their own reactions — hurt, anger, withdrawal, denial — on hold and listen. Their reactions are not important right now.

3. Spend time with your teen

Teens usually attempt suicide between 3:00 p.m. and midnight and often when someone else is in the house. If you think that suicide is impending, don't leave your teen alone. Don't leave the opportunity to kill himself available to him. Don't leave the means, the gun, the poisons, the rope where he can get them.

4. Get help

Counseling for your teen, yourself, and your family can help. It is, at the very least, evidence to your teen that you care enough to try to get help. Counselors are not always effective. Those that are effective make a tremendous difference to the family.

Find a friend to talk to so that you have some relief from the anxieties that your family situation is causing. Keep calling the crisis center for advice and encouragement. Continue to assess your teen and the family situation for months.

5. Stay involved

Stay involved with a suicidal teen for at least three months after the suicide crisis. Suicide takes energy, planning, organization, and courage. Often teens wait some time after a first crisis to try again.

They wait until they are feeling more energetic. Continue to listen, to be available for talking.

e. BLAMING THE TEEN

It is tempting to isolate the problem to the teen who tried suicide. "She always had trouble." "She never seems to cope." But the teen is not an alien living in a strange environment. Your teen is part of your family and a product of the family's interactions. The problem is the whole family's problem. The family must find healthy ways to live.

It is alarmingly common for parents to discount a first suicide attempt as an aberration that won't be repeated. They often underrate their teen's despair and deal with the suicide attempt by denying its impact. They withdraw from involvement with their teen.

The rationale for this detached attitude is encompassed in statements such as "She's old enough to look after herself." "I can't do anything with her." "She's chosen that way of life, she can deal with it." "She was only looking for attention."

The conviction that their teen was "only looking for attention" seems to be an effective way of denying the seriousness of the attempt. Parents, doctors, teachers, and nurses use this term "looking for attention" as if the teen has had a minor temper tantrum and can now be ignored. By trying to categorize the suicide attempt as "not serious," they excuse themselves from doing anything to help.

By labeling the suicide attempt as attention-getting, parents excuse themselves from concern and effort. The implication is that if parents paid any attention to the suicide attempt, they would only be making their teen worse. Therefore, their inattention and lack of help is cloaked in the motivation of a "concerned parent."

Their reason for adopting this attitude may be to protect themselves from facing the problem. Such an attitude on the part of the parents exacerbates the teen's isolation and despair and makes a second suicide attempt probable.

What do you do when suicide is imminent? If you have assessed your teenager and you are convinced that suicide is an immediate plan, there are some emergency measures that you should put in place.

f. IN AN EMERGENCY SITUATION

1. Before an attempt

Your first concern is your teen's safety. You need to protect him from harm. That may mean taking your teen to the hospital for advice on the severity of his suicidal tendencies.

Follow your own intuitive knowledge as well as your logical assessment of how serious your teen's problems are. If you feel he is desperate, you are probably right. At this time, if your teen insists to the point of yelling and screaming that he wants you to leave him alone, and you know that you shouldn't, don't. Your teen is out of control. He feels a desperate need to escape, and you must take control of the situation firmly with more authority than you feel.

If you are wrong and the situation is not as desperate as you have assessed, if your teen is not immediately suicidal and everyone, your teen, the doctor, the hospital staff, and your spouse, think you have been emotional and irrational, you will only risk your own feelings, not your child's life. You may feel embarrassed by "over-reacting," but that is far less a problem in your life than feeling remorse because you didn't act. Even if you did not assess the situation correctly and your teen was not as desperate as you thought, he will have learned that you truly care about him, that you cared enough to stay with him and to prevent his suicide. If you don't take action, he will be sure you don't care.

Taking action may mean taking all potentially lethal objects from the house: medications, including A.S.A., ropes, guns, razors, poisons, household cleaners, and alcohol. Alcohol in combination with other drugs can be lethal. Your teen knows all the possible hiding places in your house so take all the dangerous materials away — to your office or to a neighbor's.

In an emergency situation, concentrate on your child. Do not say, "I won't let you commit suicide. It's a silly thing to do," or make statements that are judgmental, belittling, or moralizing. He already knows all that. He feels he is a burden, a nuisance, in the way. Do not give him rational arguments why he should not commit suicide; he will have more and better arguments why he should. Tell him that you won't let him commit suicide because he is worthwhile and you care about him. Repeat this as often as you like, but don't get into any sort of yelling match or horrified judging. Remember, he is worth saving and you are going to help him.

If you don't know who to call for help in your community, call the crisis center and ask them for advice. It is often easier to tell your problems to a stranger than a relative or friend. You are more likely to trust their assessment of the situation and to take their advice. Many people call their doctor at this time but general practitioners are not necessarily informed about suicide prevention. The crisis center is. It is a resource that specializes in suicide prevention, and it has a list of competent resource personnel in the community. It is also open 24 hours a day and can give you "after hours" help.

If you think your teen is so unsafe that even your presence won't prevent suicide, take her to the emergency ward of the hospital. If you have a choice of hospitals, call the crisis center and ask which one to use. Some hospitals handle suicidal teens more effectively than others. Once at the hospital, stay with your teen. Every person, man, woman, or child, needs an advocate in the hospital system to ensure that they get good care. Teenagers are often subjected to verbal abuse in the emergency ward by the hospital staff. This is far less likely to happen if you are there. Many nurses and doctors do not understand the problems of suicidal teenagers and some can be judgmental, critical, and cruel.

The medical profession gets little education in suicidal patients, and many medical people seem to embrace the attitude that "suicides are a waste of medical time." Nurses and doctors sometimes feel that if they make the teen's treatment uncomfortable enough, even painful enough, the teen won't come back. Often, this strengthens the teen's resolve to avoid the hospital in the future, thus cutting out another resource that might help him.

Stay with your teen until you have worked out with her and the hospital staff a satisfactory plan that will keep her safe in the immediate future. Do not assume that no suicides occur in the hospital, that your teen will be properly supervised and have someone to talk to. The chances are that no one will help her. She may be left unsupervised for long enough to kill herself. Before you leave, find out what steps the hospital staff will take to make sure your teen is safe.

2. After an attempt

If you discover your teen after she has tried suicide, after she has swallowed the pills, tried to hang herself or shoot herself, emergency care is essential.

If she has swallowed pills, call the Poison Control Center (the telephone number is on the inside of the telephone book) and tell them what pills and how many your daughter took. Try to induce vomiting. The sooner you can get the pills up, the better. Once at the hospital, stay with your teen until you are sure she is safe from immediate harm.

After life-saving measures, when her life is no longer in immediate jeopardy, talk over plans for family counseling. This is the time when motivation is highest. Both you and your teen can see the need for outside help. Resist the temptation to dismiss this suicide episode as a "one-time phenomenon." Resist the temptation to see this episode in isolation from your normal family functioning.

This suicide attempt is a result of your family's way of functioning, not something that has occurred without cause. Look on this suicide episode as a warning of future attempts. The percentage of those who repeat suicide attempts is high enough to motivate parents to change their family's patterns. Now is your chance to start communication. Now is the time to find a good counselor and work with him or her to help your whole family.

It may take a great deal of your time and energy to get an emergency appointment with a psychiatrist. Call the crisis center for help. Do not assume that the crisis center is *only* for those who are suicidal, or that it is a center for those without finances or those without "friends in high places." The crisis center is a center for those in trouble, and that is all of us. They will respond to your problem. They will go over your teen's symptoms with you and get you the name and phone number of someone who can help.

g. WHAT DO YOU DO IF YOUR TEEN DIES IN SUICIDE?

A teen dying in suicide is such a dreadful event that most people have an immediate compassion for the parents and family. At the same time, society does blame parents for a teen suicide. Few would say so directly to the parents, but there is an unspoken acceptance of the idea that the parents should have prevented the teen's death. Parents are convinced of this themselves.

Siblings also feel that they should have stopped this brother or sister. It is often true that parents may have been able to stop a suicidal teen, so the tremendous guilt parents and siblings feel over the teen's death is based on fact. That makes it very hard. This is not a contrived guilt; this is a real guilt.

Parents and siblings have trouble forgiving themselves for not being perfect. Sometimes parents are judgmental, critical, indifferent, and abusive. But often they are not. They are no more incompetent as parents than most of us. I was surprised when I interviewed the teenagers to find that many of their parents did and said the things most parents would think were appropriate but that teens thought were devastating. It isn't possible to be perfect.

Because most teen suicides can be prevented, given understanding, early intervention, a listening ear, and an active response to cries for help, parents and siblings must deal with an overwhelming sense of remorse. After a death by suicide in the family, you must remember that you and the rest of your family are vulnerable to the idea of suicide and need counseling and care not only to deal with the death of the teen family member, but to prevent another family member from trying suicide.

Again the crisis center is one place to get a referral for a counselor. Your church may have a counselor who is very good at dealing with grieving. Find out if he or she will help you with your guilt over the suicide and will help with changing the family patterns so that no one else will see suicide as a way out.

Some cities offer "survivor's groups" where mutual help is given by others in similar states of loss and remorse. Groups such as these can help families work through their problems. There is no comfort in saying that parents will adjust and be able to forget the pain of a child's suicide. They will never forget it, but they may be able in time to live with it. And they may be able to help rule out suicide as a choice for the surviving family members.

Doing the general assessment on Worksheet #5 should help you evaluate what is happening in your family.

WORKSHEET #4
SUICIDE SIGNS AND SYMPTOMS

General

1. Depression

    Do you feel that your teen is unhappy? _____

    _____

    Do you see changes in his/her behavior that cause you worry?

    _____

2. Feelings of inadequacy, incompetence

    Can you assess this by listening and watching? _____

    _____

    Does he tell you he/she feels worthless, does he/she say he/she isn't "good enough," or that he/she can't do many things? _____

    _____

3. Feelings of helplessness

    Do you think your teen feels he/she has no control over life?

    _____

    Does he/she say "No matter what I do, it won't work"?

    _____

    Does he/she assume he/she is going to fail?

    _____

4. Feelings of hopelessness

    Do you think your teen feels there is no future for him/her?

    _____

    Does your teen talk about the future at all, does he/she make any plans? _____

    _____

In Particular

Have you noticed some or many of the following:

1. School failure. Are comments coming home that indicate your teen is "not trying," "inattentive in class," "does not complete assignments," "is the class clown," "disruptive in class," "does not participate in class," "has missed many classes"?

   _____

2. Irrational behavior such as temper tantrums, exaggerated hurt over what parents consider small matters, elaborate sarcasm and vicious remarks aimed at hurting others.

   _____

3. Eating problems. Attempting to diet into pencil shape or gorging into a melon shape.

   _____

4. Sleeping problems. Staying up late every night and waking early.

   _____

5. Changes in social life. Becoming obsessively involved with a boyfriend/girlfriend to the exclusion of all other friends. Or, becoming isolated socially, seeing no one, socializing with no one. Or seeking the company of the fringes of teen society, the bizarre, the "losers," the misfits.

   _____

6. Increasing use of alcohol and drugs.

   _____

7. Increasing need for perfect grades, perfect achievements, no tolerance of failure.

   _____

8. Increasing accidents/illnesses.

   _____

Signs and Symptoms of Impending Suicide

1. The above behaviors increasing in severity.

2. Preoccupation with death, in writing, poetry, songs, and paintings.

3. Giving away possessions, writing a will.

4. Talking about death in an oblique way, "I won't be here," "You'd be better off without me," "There isn't any future for me," "Nothing's any use, I won't be around long."

5. An additional loss, a boyfriend/girlfriend abandoning the teen, or leaving town, father or mother separating from the family, graduation from high school and subsequent breakup of social group or "usual" life, move to another community with loss of the familiar, death of a relative, friend, someone in the school, even death of an celebrity especially if that death was by suicide, *any* event that is considered a loss by the teen.

WORKSHEET #5
GENERAL ASSESSMENT

This worksheet may help you look more objectively at your teen and at his or her place in the family.

1. What do you notice about your teen that you find —

   upsetting _____

   _____

   unacceptable _____

   _____

   worrisome _____

   _____

2. What do you notice that you find —

   admirable _____

   _____

   interesting _____

   _____

3. What do you wish your teen would change —

   at home _____

   _____

   at school _____

   _____

   in the community (socially) _____

   _____

4. What do you hope your teen will continue to do —

   at home _____

   _____

   at school _____

   _____

   in the community (socially) _____

   _____

5. Communication

Your teen —

☐ talks easily about all subjects

☐ usually tells me his/her worries

☐ occasionally tells me his/her worries

☐ never tells me his/her worries or fears but will talk about other subjects

☐ seldom talks to me

☐ is verbally abusive to me

6. What does your teenager see as stress?

_____

_____

_____

7. What does he/she see as helpful to alleviate stress?

☐ yelling

☐ arguing

☐ shutting himself/herself in the bedroom

☐ playing music (either listening or practicing an instrument)

☐ watching T.V.

☐ partying with alcohol

☐ partying with drugs

☐ verbally abusing others (sadistically, sarcastically, viciously)

☐ physically abusing others (fighting)

☐ physical exercise (working out in the gym, sports, jogging)

☐ talking to friends

☐ talking to professionals (psychologist, teacher, doctor, counselor)

☐ talking to parent(s)

☐ becoming sick (physical ailments related to stress)

8. How does your teenager see himself in relationship

   — to the family?

   ❏ wanted

   ❏ ignored

   — to other teens?

   ❏ accepted

   ❏ not accepted

9. Who in your extended family could help?

   _____

   _____

   _____

10. Who else would you call if you wanted help with your teen?

    ❏ minister

    ❏ your friend

    ❏ teacher

    ❏ your teen's friend

    ❏ doctor

    ❏ psychologists

    ❏ social worker

    ❏ public health nurse

11. Does your teen know this person?

    _____

    _____

12

FINALLY

We worry about them; educate them; cram vitamins into them; give them warm socks and hot milk; teach them; caution them; continually explain; give them birthday presents, outings, trips, time, energy, and love in the great effort of bringing them up to be confident, outgoing, intelligent, sensible people.

When we see that they are unhappy and have low self-esteem, we are often both worried and angry that what we have done isn't enough. Very often, our intentions are admirable, but our skills are weak.

Most of us didn't consider suicide as an escape when we were young and we don't understand why our children do, especially when it seems as though their lives are so much more interesting and fulfilling than ours were.

In many cases, we practice the habit of denial — I don't want my child to be suicidal, so she isn't — ignoring the signs and symptoms she shows, the evidence of suicide in the neighborhood and school, the statistics for her age group.

If, after reading this book, you understand that suicide is a threat to everyone's children, that the signs and symptoms of impending suicide require immediate attention, that parents often need new skills, especially listening skills, to deal with the situation, and that there is help in the community for your teen and yourself, then you have what you need to make changes.

There is no magic word, gesture, or incantation that makes suicide go away. But if we learn to truly listen to our teens, their chances of trying suicide decrease dramatically.

Learning to listen, uncritically and nonjudgmentally, while accepting, encouraging, and trying to understand them, is the single most important thing we can do.

APPENDIX
FURTHER RESOURCES

a. BOOKS

Alvarez, A. *The Savage God: A Study of Suicide.* New York: Random House, 1972.

Callwood, June. *Emotions: What They Are and How They Affect Us.* Toronto: Doubleday of Canada, 1986.

Canadian Mental Health Association. *Listen to Me: A Guide for Youth on Depression and Suicide.*

Centers for Disease Control. *Suicide: Surveillance.* Atlanta: U.S. Department of Health & Human Services. Public Health Service, 1985.

Colt, George Howe. *The Enigma of Suicide.* New York: Summit Books, 1991.

Coopersmith, Stanley. *The Antecedents of Self-Esteem.* San Francisco: W. H. Freeman, 1967.

Diekstra, R.F.W. and K. Hawton. *Suicide in Adolescence.* Dordrecht, Netherlands: Martinus Nijhoff, 1987.

Evoy, John J. *The Rejected: Psychological Consequences of Parental Rejection.* University Park: Pennsylvania State University Press, 1982.

Farberow, Norman L., ed. *The Many Faces of Suicide, Indirect Self-Destruction.* New York: McGraw-Hill, 1980.

Giovacchini, Peter. *The Urge to Die: Why Young People Commit Suicide.* New York: Macmillan, 1981.

Gordon, Sol. *When Living Hurts.* New York: Union of American Hebrew Congregations, 1985.

Harter, S. "Developmental Perspectives on the Self-System." In *Handbook of Child Psychology,* ed. P. Mussen. Vol. IV, *Socialization, Personality and Social Development.* New York: John Wiley & Sons, 1983.

Hendin, Herbert. *Suicide in America*. New York: W.W. Norton, 1982.

Keir, Norman. *I Can't Face Tomorrow*. Rochester: Thorsons Publishing Groups, 1986.

Klagsbrun, Francine. *Too Young to Die*. Boston: Houghton Mifflin, 1976.

Lecky, P. *Self-Consistency: A Theory of Personality*. U.S.A.: The Shoe String Press, 1961.

Lester, David. *Why People Kill Themselves: A 1980's Summary of Research Findings on Suicidal Behavior*. 2nd ed. Springfield, Ill.: Charles C. Thomas, 1983.

Lukas, C. and H.M. Seiden. *Silent Grief: Living in the Wake of Suicide*. New York: Charles Scribner's Sons, 1987.

Mack, John, and Holly Hickler. *Vivienne: The Life and Suicide of an Adolescent Girl*. Boston: Little, 1983.

Maris, Ronald W. *Pathways to Suicide: A Survey of Self-Destructive Behaviors*. Baltimore: Johns Hopkins University Press, 1981.

Peck, M.L., N.L. Farberow and R.E. Litman. *Youth Suicide*. New York: Springer, 1985.

Pfeffer, C.R. *The Suicidal Child*. New York: Guilford, 1986.

Reynolds, David K., and Norman L. Farberow. *The Family Shadow: Sources of Suicide and Schizophrenia*. Berkeley: University of California Press, 1981.

Robinson, Rita. *Survivors of Suicide*. Santa Monica: IBS Press, 1989.

Rosenfeld, Linda, and Marilynne Prupas. *Left Alive: After a Suicide Death in the Family*. Springfield, Ill.: Charles C. Thomas, 1984.

Sanderson, J. D. *How to Stop Worrying About Your Kids*. New York: W. W. Norton, 1978.

Scarf, Maggie. *Intimate Partners: Patterns in Love and Marriage*. New York: Random House, 1987.

Sirgy, M. Joseph. Self-Congruity: Toward a Theory of Personality and Cybernetics. New York: Praeger, 1986.

Sudak, H.S. and N.B. Rushford. *Suicide in the Young*. Boston: John Wright, 1984.

Tavris, Carol. *Anger: The Misunderstood Emotion.* New York: Simon and Schuster, 1982.

Victoroff, V.M. *The Suicidal Patient: Recognition, Intervention, Management.* Oradell, N.J.: Medical Economics Books, 1983.

Viorst, Judith. *Necessary Losses.* New York: Fawcett, 1987.

Wells, L. Edward, and G. Marwell. *Self-Esteem: Its Conceptualization and Measurement.* Beverly Hills: Sage Publications, 1976.

White, Bowden. *Everything to Live For.* New York: Poseidon Press, 1985.

Wrobleski, Adina. *Suicide: Survivors, A Guide for Those Left Behind.* Minneapolis: Afterwords Publishing, 1991.

b. ARTICLES

Andrus, Jon K., et. al. "Surveillance of attempted suicide among adolescents in Oregon." *The American Journal of Public Health, August, 1991.*

Bagley, Christopher, and Richard Ramsay. "Problems and Priorities in Research on Suicidal Behavior: An Overview with Canadian Implications." *Canadian Journal of Community Mental Health* 4, no. 1 (Spring 1985).

Barish, Sidney. "Responding to adolescent suicide: a multi-faceted plan." *NASSSP Bulletin.* November, 1991.

Edwards, Thomas K. "Giving students reasons for wanting to live." *Education Digest.* March, 1989.

Etlin, Melissa. "Preventing Teen Suicide: Programs that Work." *NEA Today.* May-June, 1990.

Hendin, H. "Growing up Dead: Student Suicide." *American Journal of Psychotherapy* 29(3) 1975 327-338.

Kaufman, Joan, et. al. "Adolescents who Attempt Suicide." *The Journal of the American Medical Association.* June 5, 1991.

Konopka, Gisela. "Adolescent Suicide." *Exceptional Children* 49, no. 5 (February 1983): 390-94.

National Task Force on Suicide in Canada. "Suicide in Canada." *Report of the National Task Force on Suicide in Canada* (1987).

New England Journal of Medicine. "The Impact of Suicide in Television Movies." *The New England Journal of Medicine* (11 September 1986): 690.

Pettifor, J., D. Perry, B. Plowman, and S. Pitcher. "Risk Factors Prediction: Childhood and Adolescent Suicides." *Journal of Child Care* 1, no. 3 (January 1983): 17-49.

Rubenstein, Judit L. et. al. "Suicidal Behavior in 'Normal' Adolescents: Risk and Protective Factors." *The American Journal of Orthopsychiatry*. January, 1989.

Westwood, Michael. "The Health of Canadian Youth: A Developmental Perspective." *Health Promotion* (1987).

Zimmerman, Joy. "Teenage Suicide." *Pacific Sun* (10-16 April 1987).

c. FILMS

Before It's Too Late. Walt Disney Educational Media, 1985.

But Jack Was A Good Driver. CRM Productions, Scarborough, Ontario, 1974.

Childhood's End. R. Lang, Kensington Communications, TV Ontario, 1981.

Conspiracy of Silence. Canadian Broadcasting Corporation, 1981.

Dead Serious. MTI Film & Video, 1987.

Listen to Me. Canadian Mental Health Association, 1986.

Troubled Teens. Mission Community Services, 1990

Urgent Messages. Vancouver Crisis Centre, 1982.

d. RESOURCES

Suicide Information and Education Centre
201-1615 10th Avenue S.W.
Calgary, Alberta
T3C 0J7
Telephone: (403) 245-3900

The Suicide Information and Education Centre can provide you with almost any other source you wish.

e. OTHER SOURCES

Crisis Intervention and Suicide Prevention Centre
    for Greater Vancouver
1946 East Broadway
Vancouver, B.C.
V6J 1Z2
Telephone: (604) 733-1171

Toronto Distress Centre
10 Trinity Square
Toronto, Ontario
M5B 1G1
Telephone: (416) 598-0166

Helpline
Coberg and Oxford
Halifax, Nova Scotia
B3H 3J5
Telephone: (902) 422-2048

Richmond Health Clinic
Box 2000
Charlottetown, P.E.I.
C1A 7N8
Telephone: (902) 368-4430

Peekisweta, Let's Talk Agency
General Delivery
Wabasca, Alberta
T0G 0T0
Telephone: (403) 891-3640

Canadian Association for Suicide Prevention
Box 56, Station K
Toronto, Ontario
M4P 2G1

American Association of Suicidology
2459 South Ash
Denver Colorado 80222
Telephone: (303) 692-0985

ORDERING INFORMATION

All prices are subject to change without notice. Books are available in book, department, and stationery stores. If you cannot buy the book through a store, please use this order form. (Please print)

IN CANADA

Please send your order to the nearest location:
Self-Counsel Press, 1481 Charlotte Road,
North Vancouver, B. C. V7J 1H1

Self-Counsel Press, #8-2283 Argentia Road,
Mississauga, Ontario L5A 5Z2
Please add 7% GST to the cost of the books.
Please add $2.68 ($2.50 postage and handling, 18¢ GST).

IN THE U.S.A.

Please send your order to:
Self-Counsel Press Inc., 1704 N. State Street,
Bellingham, WA 98225
Please add $2.50 for postage & handling.
WA residents please add 7.8% sales tax

Name_____

Address_____

_____

Charge to:
❑Visa   ❑ MasterCard

Account Number _____

Validation Date_____Expiry Date _____

Signature_____

❑Check here for a free catalogue.

YES, please send me
_____copies of **No-Gimmick Guide to Managing Stress**, $11.95
_____copies of **Family Ties That Bind**, $8.95